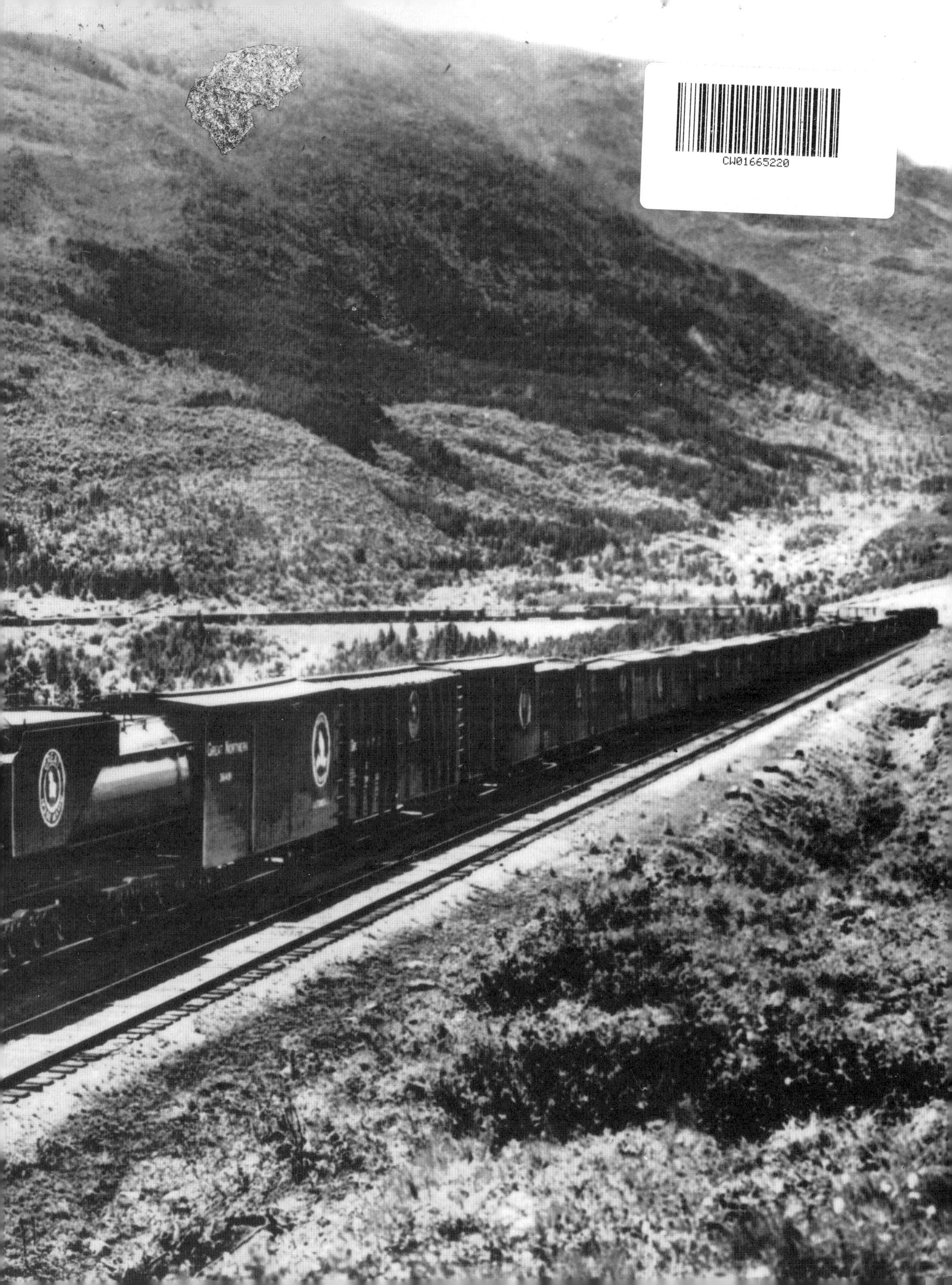
Great Northern

GREAT NORTHERN
the New Empire Builder
custom-built for pleasant, faster travel
A new generation of a long-distinguished fleet of transcontinental trains—Great Northern's New EMPIRE BUILDERS. The first modern, sleeping car-coach trains built since the war, the New EMPIRE BUILDERS inaugurate the first streamliner service between Chicago and the Pacific Northwest on a daily 45-hour schedule. These sleek, colorful, diesel-drawn trains are custom-built for comfortable, refreshing travel. New style coaches . . . duplex roomettes . . . spacious bedrooms . . . cheerful lounges . . . gay coffee shops . . . and charming dining cars with Great Northern's famous food service. The New EMPIRE BUILDERS—modern trains designed for modern travelers.
New design duplex roomettes . . . ideal for the passenger who desires complete privacy and comfort.
New style Day-Nite coaches . . . more room for each passenger, more comfort and convenience.
GREAT NORTHERN RAILWAY
Serves the Best of the Great Northwest
PACIFIC OCEAN
WASH.
OREGON
IDAHO
MONTANA
SASKATCHEWAN
N. DAKOTA
S. DAKOTA
MINN.
WISC.
IOWA
ONTARIO
QUEBEC
LAKE SUPERIOR
ATLANTIC OCEAN
TO CALIFORNIA
Route of the New Empire Builder

EMPIRE BUILDER

GREAT NORTHERN
EMPIRE BUILDER

BILL YENNE

MBI

ACKNOWLEDGMENTS

I would like to thank Suzanne Burris of the Burlington Northern Santa Fe Corporation for supplying historic photos from the BNSF Archives, Dan Engstrom of Amtrak for supplying current *Empire Builder* materials, J. Craig Thorpe for sharing his paintings, Scott Leonard of the National Association of Railroad Passengers for supplying timetable data, Bev Tracy at the Great Northern Railway Historical Society for supplying info on Omaha Orange, and Dennis Pernu of MBI Publishing Company for giving me the opportunity to assemble this book on a train that is such an indelible part of my memory.

First published in 2005 by MBI, an imprint of MBI Publishing Company, Galtier Plaza, Suite 200, 380 Jackson Street, St. Paul, MN 55101-3885 USA

ISBN 0-7603-1847-6
Editorial: Amy Glaser
Design: LeAnn Kuhlmann
Printed in China

On the endpapers: *Author collection*
On the frontispiece: This 1947 advertisement for the New *Empire Builder* celebrated the style and comfort of new passenger cars. The artist needed to take no license in making the E7A (E-7) diesel look fast and streamlined. For the next two decades, the Great Northern used paintings of the train in the Rockies to promote its *Empire Builder*. *Author collection*
On the title page: An 11-car *Empire Builder* crosses the rolling hills of the American West under the motive power of a pair of Electro-Motive Division E7A diesels. Placed into service in 1947, the New *Empire Builder* introduced the Omaha Orange and Pullman Green color scheme that was the signature look of the great streamliner during its golden age. *Author collection*
On the table of contents page: *Author collection*
On the back cover(TOP): This is what it looks like inside the *Empire Builder* Great Dome lounge car. The plush seats guaranteed a comfortable ride, and the virtually limitless windows guaranteed a sensational view of whatever there was to see as the streamliner zipped across the continent. The modern Amtrak Superliners afford a reasonable facsimile of the experience, but there is nothing like a Budd car. Five of the original six still exist in the twenty-first century. *BNSF Archives* **(BOTTOM):** In 1955, the *Empire Builder* reached its apogee with the delivery of the dome cars built by the Budd Company. To celebrate the Great Domes, Great Northern produced a series of advertisements featuring fanciful images of Western landscapes. This illustration suggests the majesty of Glacier National Park, but there really was no place on the route where the *Empire Builder* got quite this close to mountains of this stature. *Author collection*

GLACIER PARK
TRANSPORT CO.
CAR C
SEAT 3-456
BELTON
WESTBOUND
TRAIN
CAR NO. 36
SPACE Bedroom C

GREAT NORTHERN
RAILWAY CO.
1950
PASS
B 42594
K.L.Clark...
Div.Engr.
CMSt.P&P R.R.Co.
UNTIL DECEMBER 31, 1950, UNLESS OTHERWISE SPECIFIED
VALID WHEN COUNTERSIGNED BY
A. C. BERG OR L. J. BERGSTROM
COUNTERSIGNED BY
VICE PRESIDENT
THIS PASS ACCEPTED BY ME
SUBJECT TO CONDITIONS ON BACK

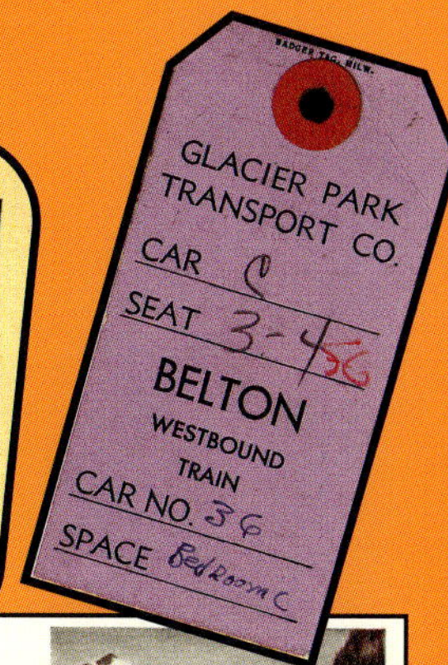
GLACIER PARK
TRANSPORT CO.
CAR C
SEAT 3-456
BELTON
WESTBOUND
TRAIN
CAR NO. 36
SPACE Bedroom C

CONTENTS

Rolling
through the Rockies
YOUR uniformed sons and daughters, traveling over America on the Great Northern Railway, cross the Continental Divide almost without knowing it. The train follows a natural route—easy as a game trail—through the scenic grandeur of the Montana Rockies. That is Marias Pass!
At the top of the pass—at Summit, Montana—they see a statue of its discoverer, John F. Stevens, who still is living. In December, 1889, Stevens found a broad, natural corridor through the Rockies, which provided the lowest (5,213 feet) and easiest railway pass in the northern United States.
Stevens' discovery not only gave Great Northern its low-altitude pass through the mountains, it also led to establishment of Glacier National Park—the only national park on the main line of an American railway.
Manpower, firepower and supplies for America and her Allies are rolling through the Rockies faster and on time because Marias Pass affords swifter, safer handling of trains.
Marias Pass helps make Great Northern dependable—a vital artery to Victory.
GREAT NORTHERN
RAILWAY
ROUTE OF THE EMPIRE BUILDER
BETWEEN THE GREAT LAKES AND THE PACIFIC

GREAT NORTHERN
RAILWAY

EMPIRE
BUILDER

GREAT NORTHERN
RAILWAY

Introduction

The Great Northern Railway system was traditionally known as "The Route of the Empire Builder," a clever double entendre that paid tribute to both a man and a train. James Jerome (Jim) Hill was a visionary entrepreneur who came of age in a time when America celebrated such men. He was not simply an empire builder. He was *the* Empire Builder.

Ironically, although Jim Hill devoted his life to the settlement of the immense territory between the Great Lakes and the Pacific Northwest, he never knew the train that traversed it. The *Empire Builder*, destined to be the premier transcontinental passenger train of the Great Northern Railway and the principal passenger train between Chicago and Seattle, made its first run in 1929. On its run that day and on subsequent runs nearly every day for more than seven ensuing decades, it crossed what once were staggering natural barriers, but were no longer barriers because of Hill.

The route of the *Empire Builder* was, as the Great Northern's copywriters mused, a "Clean, Cinderless, Scenic Route" and later a "Great Dome Route," but it was more than that. It was a triumphant and heroic route. It crossed the great continent from Lake Michigan to Puget Sound, surmounting the glacier-bound Rocky Mountains by way of a pass whose discovery was a monument to heroic exploration. It crossed the snow-crested Cascades by way of a tunnel that was a monument to heroic engineering and the brute force of the steel-driving man.

The Empire Builder had envisioned passenger service on this route, and he saw it become a reality in his own lifetime through his legendary *Oriental Limited*, the precursor to the *Empire Builder*. In observing the course of his new passenger line, Hill was inspired by the massive beauty of the place that George Bird Grinnell had called the "Crown of the Continent." The Empire Builder's vision turned this magnificent wilderness which straddles the Continental Divide into Glacier National Park. He was the catalyst for the creation of the only national park in the United States that was touched directly by a transcontinental passenger railroad—*his* road. Of course, most visitors to Glacier National Park needed to buy a ticket on the Great Northern to get to the park, but without the Great Northern few people would have had a chance to see Glacier National Park during the early decades of its existence.

The eastbound *Empire Builder* crosses the Continental Divide at Marias Pass in 1960. Across Bear Creek, riders pause to water their horses and watch. Little Dog Mountain and Summit Mountain in Glacier National Park form a majestic background.

Hill gave Glacier National Park to the travelling public, just as he had given the vast farmlands of North Dakota and Montana to an earlier generation of settlers. He had given these homesteaders the transportation to get to the land and to send their produce to market. He created an infrastructure in a corner of the continent that could never have developed without him. As the nation matured, he developed tourism.

When Hill was gone, the railroad that he founded gave him immortality as the namesake for a new train that wrote another chapter in the history of that great land. Indeed, just as the Great Northern survived for half a century after the death of the Empire Builder, the *Empire Builder* survived into the twenty-first century, long after the Great Northern was no more.

The Great Northern Railway was one of the half-dozen greatest railroads of American history, yet its own history is incomplete without telling the story of the Empire Builder and the *Empire Builder*. Nor is the history of the northwestern tier of the United States complete without the story of these three: the man, his railroad, and that railroad's signature train.

This is that story.

In 1945 and 1947, the Great Northern took delivery of 13 Electro-Motive Division E7A diesels to use for the postwar edition of the *Empire Builder*. *Author collection*

This pictographic map from the 1930s highlights the route of the *Empire Builder* and its sister train, the *Oriental Limited*. Essentially, the *Empire Builder* ran between Chicago and Seattle, with additional service to Portland out of Spokane. Connecting lines controlled by the Great Northern are shown in red. Glacier National Park in Montana and the adjoining Waterton Lakes National Park in Alberta were the signature tourist destinations for the *Empire Builder*. *Author collection*

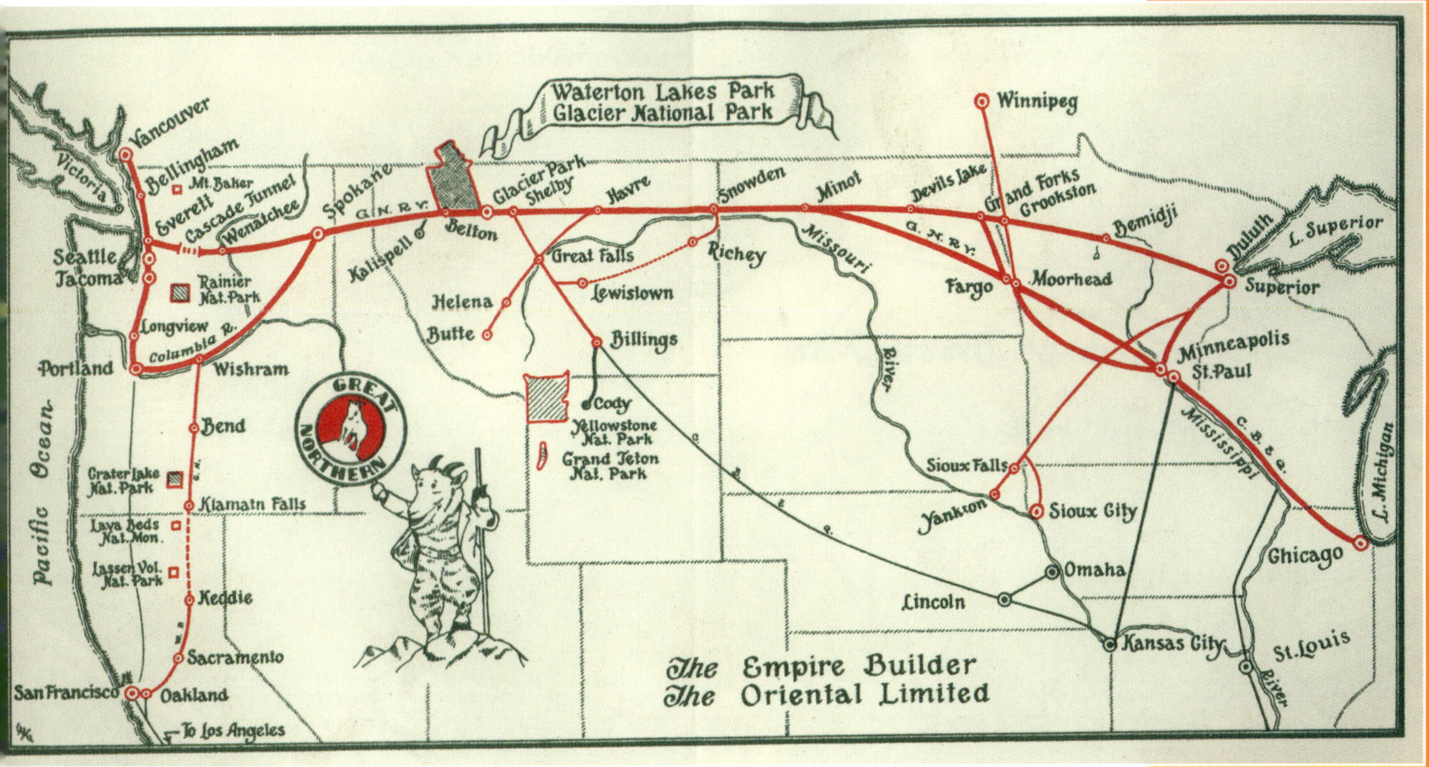

4 NEW GREAT DOMES
ON THE WORLD-FAMOUS
EMPIRE BUILDER
GREAT NORTHERN
EMPIRE BUILDER
MORE LUXURY DOME SEATS FOR THE MOST SCENIC MILES ON ANY TRAIN BETWEEN CHICAGO · TWIN CITIES · SPOKANE · SEATTLE · PORTLAND
GO GREAT...GO GREAT NORTHERN
There now are 147 topside seats in the Great Domes on the distinguished Empire Builder—the most dome seats on any streamliner between Chicago and Pacific Northwest cities. And, there's *no extra fare* for helping yourself to a grandstand seat for the *extra wonderful sightseeing* in Great Northern country. Three luxurious Great Domes in the coach section of the Empire Builder, plus an exciting, colorful full-length Great Dome in the Pullman section, with a smart lounge on the lower deck. Go Great Northern—and you'll go great!
VANCOUVER
WINNIPEG
EVERETT
SEATTLE
TACOMA
WENATCHEE
SPOKANE
MINOT
GRAND FORKS
DULUTH
SUPERIOR
GREAT FALLS
FARGO
ST. PAUL
MINNEAPOLIS
PORTLAND
HELENA
BILLINGS
BUTTE
CHICAGO
TO CALIFORNIA
GO THE GREAT DOME ROUTE
CONNECTIONS TO AND FROM
CALIFORNIA
GREAT NORTHERN RAILWAY
For information: Write Passenger Dept., Great Northern, St. Paul 1, Minn.

Opposite: In 1955, the *Empire Builder* reached its apogee with the delivery of the Budd Company dome cars. To celebrate the Great Domes, Great Northern produced a series of advertisements featuring fanciful images of Western landscapes. This illustration suggests the majesty of Glacier National Park, but there really was no place on the route where the *Empire Builder* got quite this close to mountains of this stature. *Author collection*

The Great Northern Railway extended the courtesy of a pass on its lines to K. L. Clark, a division engineer on the Chicago, Milwaukee, St. Paul & Pacific. The latter road had lines that paralleled the Great Northern to the south. *Author collection*

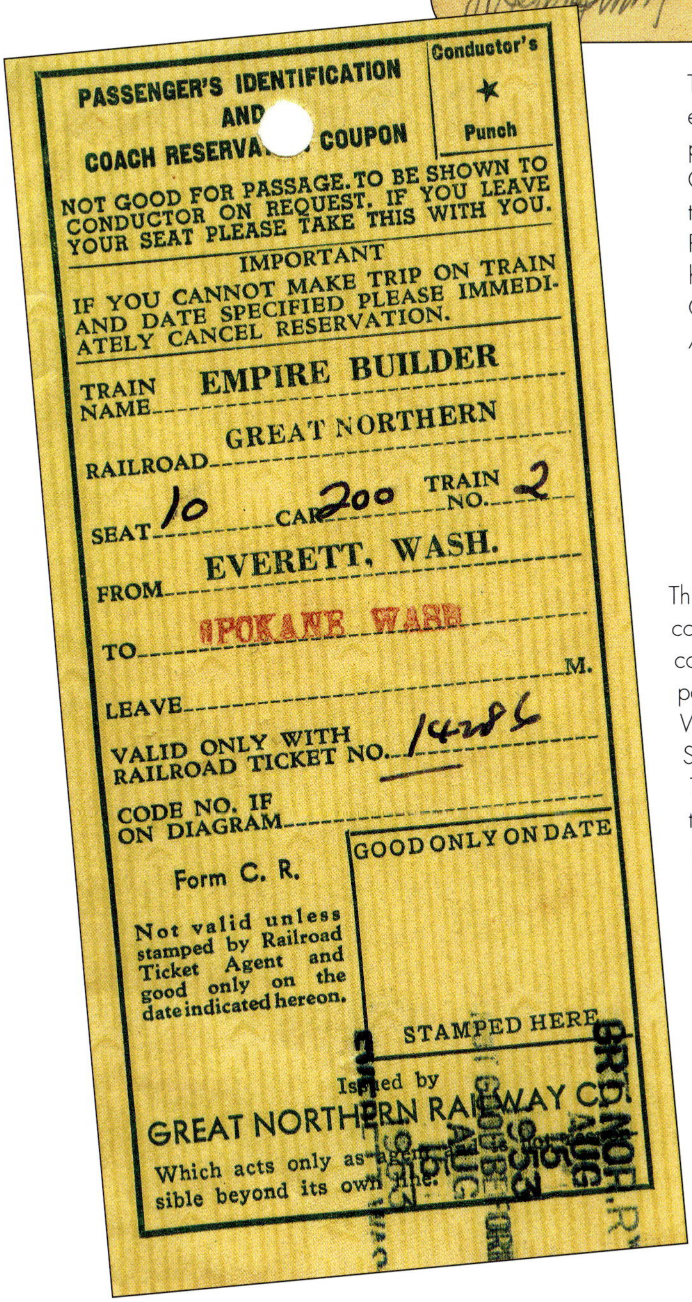

This *Empire Builder* coach reservation coupon took its passenger from Everett, Washington, to Spokane in August 1953. Not only was the *Empire Builder* the railroad of choice for long transcontinental trips, but it was also useful for intrastate traffic across the northern tier of the northwestern United States. *Author collection*

One

James Jerome Hill

Before there was an *Empire Builder*, there was *the* Empire Builder. All stories need their protagonist, and in this tale it is James Jerome Hill, the visionary and entrepreneur who was known in the late nineteenth century, and always will be, as the "Empire Builder."

James Jerome Hill was born of Irish ancestry on September 16, 1838, in a log cabin in Canada's Ontario province. He died a multimillionaire financier in St. Paul, Minnesota, on May 29, 1916, at the age of 77. Hill's legacy was the Great Northern Railway. Of all the great railroads of the golden age of American railroading, no other so completely dominated, both economically and culturally, the corner of the country where it operated. The Great Northern is special to American history. It stands out, regal and aloof like the Rocky Mountain goat that was its emblem. In 1912, upon retiring from the company that he personified, Jim Hill said, "Most men who have really lived have had, in some shape, their great adventure. This railway is mine."

Jim Hill's great adventure began in 1856. When he was 18 years old, he left his birthplace, a farm carved from the forest near Rockwood by his parents. After his father's death, his early education was interrupted by the need for his help with the family income. Hill showed such promise, however, that the headmaster of his school, the Rockwood Academy, extended an academic scholarship. Nevertheless, the young Hill was itching to see the world beyond eastern Ontario.

Deciding that he'd like to seek his fortune as a sea captain in Oriental commerce, he headed for the Atlantic Seaboard, but he had no luck obtaining passage aboard any ship bound for the Far East. To reach the East, Hill decided to go west to the Pacific Coast. En route, he planned to visit a friend at Fort Garry—now

This is James Jerome Hill, *the* Empire Builder. Born in Ontario, he moved to St. Paul at the age of 18 and began a career in transportation. He controlled the St. Paul, Minneapolis & Manitoba Railway and turned the Great Northern Railway into the most powerful railroad on the northwestern tier of the United States. "Most men who have really lived have had, in some shape, their great adventure," Hill said. "This railway is mine." *Author collection*

The balloon-stacked *Wm. Crooks* was the first locomotive to operate on the St. Paul & Pacific Railroad, and it was the first predecessor line to the Great Northern to operate motive power. Built in 1861 by Smith & Jackson in Paterson, New Jersey, the 51-foot 4-4-0 American made its first run in June 1862. It was named for Colonel William Crooks, the railroad's chief engineer, and it carried the Number 1 for the St. Paul & Pacific, and later for the Great Northern. It operated as a Great Northern demonstration locomotive until 1962, when it was donated to the Minnesota Historical Society. *Author collection*

Winnipeg—in Manitoba, but by the time he reached St. Paul, Minnesota, the last ox cart caravan of the season had already left for the north. Hill was stuck in St. Paul for the winter, and he had to find work to tide him over until spring. He took a job as a shipping clerk in the office of a Mississippi River steamboat company. His lifelong career in transportation, and his lifelong residence in St. Paul, had begun.

Hill went on to serve as clerk for the steamboat line, calculating freight rates and learning steamboat operations. His early jobs gave him a good grounding in the problems of freight transportation, with which he would always be involved.

Meanwhile, steamboat transit was on the threshold of facing competition from a new transportation technology—railroads. At the time, most of the iron rails in North America were within a day's ride of the Atlantic, but railroad technology and its promise were spreading quickly. The Minnesota territorial legislature, eager for rail lines in its domain, had granted railroad charters as early as 1853 and had issued one in 1857 to the Minnesota & Pacific Railroad Company. The latter provided for construction of a line from Stillwater, Minnesota, on the St. Croix River, to St. Paul, St. Anthony (now Minneapolis), and Breckenridge, and another by way of St. Cloud to St. Vincent on the Canadian border. The "Pacific" in the name was merely wishful thinking. Many, if not most, of the railroads chartered in the United States with "& Pacific" at the end of their names never got near the western ocean.

The United States federal government made a land grant to the Minnesota & Pacific Railroad of six sections to the mile, which was later increased to 10 sections to the mile. Minnesota, as soon as it became the 32nd state in May 1858, helped with a bond issue, using the land grant as security. The sum of $100,000 was

allowed for every 10 miles of grading, and the same amount was allowed for every 10 miles of completed road. Under the terms of the federal grant, the line had to be completed within 10 years or the land would revert back to the United States.

Although St. Paul quickly emerged as the railroad hub of Minnesota, there was still plenty of activity in Minneapolis, as demonstrated in this 1874 photo of the Minneapolis station at Washington Avenue and Third Avenue North. The equipment pictured is from the St. Paul, Minneapolis & Manitoba Railway. *Author collection*

Building a railroad in Minnesota in the 1850s was a task easier said than done. Grading and track-laying was virtually impossible through the long frozen winters, so construction itself was a seasonal endeavor. Meanwhile, because there was no rail link to the East, locomotives and rolling stock had to be brought up the Mississippi River on barges.

The loan was exhausted in 1859, the Minnesota & Pacific Railroad went bankrupt, and it later emerged as the St. Paul & Pacific Railroad. In its new incarnation, the railroad finally completed the first 10 miles of construction in Minnesota—from St. Paul to St. Anthony—and began regular operations on July 2, 1862. The first locomotive in service was the wood-burning 4-4-0 American that was named *Wm. Crooks* after the railroad's chief engineer.

Mcanwhilc, Hill kcpt an cyc on thc ncw tcchnology from his vantagc point in the steamship industry. By now, he had become an independent freight agent and commodities broker, and was the most successful freight forwarder in St. Paul. He represented a steamboat line that connected with eastbound rails at lower Mississippi River points. In 1866, he began serving as an agent for the First Division of the St. Paul & Pacific.

Hill saw the future in coal. It was preferable to wood as a fuel for the railroads, and he began brokering coal for the St. Paul & Pacific Line. Soon, he expanded his business with former competitors as partners in the Northwestern Fuel Company. Hill's familiarity with steamships also led him into a partnership with Norman Wolfred Kittson in the operation of a fur transport steamship line, which competed successfully with the powerful Hudson's Bay Company on the Red River between

Construction crews moving up to the railhead of the St. Paul, Minneapolis & Manitoba Railway pause to pose with their dormitory cars in 1887 in western Dakota Territory (now North Dakota). They began working west in Minot on April 2 of that year and reached Helena on November 19 after building 642 miles of track. *Author collection*

Donald Alexander Smith, later Baron Strathcona and Mount Royal, backed Jim Hill in the St. Paul, Minneapolis & Manitoba venture. He was born at Forres, Moray, Scotland, and joined the Hudson's Bay Company in 1838. One of the principal financiers of the Canadian Pacific Railway, he drove its last spike in 1885. He was also a major investor in the Bank of Montreal. *Author collection*

the United States and Canada. Like Hill, Kittson was a Canadian. He had emigrated to the United States in 1834 at the age of 20, became manager of the American Fur Company in northern Minnesota, and served on the Minnesota territorial legislature from 1851 to 1855. By 1858, he was mayor of St. Paul.

Through the 1870s, the St. Paul & Pacific Railroad was constantly struggling to remain solvent. Hill watched this, but decided the problems had more to do with the specific management of this railroad than with the idea of railroads in general. When the St. Paul & Pacific Railroad fell on hard times in 1878, Hill saw an opportunity. He acquired the railroad and rehabilitated it. To facilitate his acquisition, Hill assembled a consortium of like-minded empire builders. These included Kittson and two of the most powerful and ambitious entrepreneurs in Canada. These men were George Stephen, president of the Bank of Montreal, who later became Lord Mount Stephen; and Stephen's cousin Donald Alexander Smith, the chief commissioner of the Hudson's Bay Company, who later became Lord Strathcona. The two men subsequently gained fame as pioneer railway builders in Canada through the creation of the Canadian Pacific Railway, which became the largest privately held railroad in that country.

A Highland lad who arrived in Canada from Scotland at age 18, Donald Smith had spent most of his life working for the Hudson's Bay Company, mainly in the dreary wilds of

Labrador and on the shores of Hudson Bay. In 1871, when Smith became chief commissioner of the organization he had served so long, it seemed to most men that he was settled in his life work and probably near the height of his career. However, Smith knew that his career was only beginning. After coming down from the north each year by the Red River to St. Paul on his way east, he would talk over the railway situation with Hill and Kittson. The more they talked, the greater their belief in the country and the railroad grew. However, it was a belief that few in moneyed eastern Canada shared with them.

Thirty years earlier, George Stephen, a younger cousin of Donald Smith, had left Scotland to seek his fortune in London, and after a short apprenticeship there, he joined an uncle in Montreal. Stephen rose rapidly to a foremost place in the wholesale trade of Montreal. Selling led him into manufacturing, and manufacturing into financial activities, until he became president of the Bank of Montreal in 1876.

That same year a lawsuit in connection with the bank's affairs took Stephen to Chicago. A week's adjournment left him with time on his hands, and a coin toss sent him to St. Paul instead of St. Louis to spend the week. Smith had already spoken of the project while he was in Montreal, but at that distance, caution had prevailed. Now Stephen, who had never before seen the prairie, was immensely taken with the rich, deep soil he saw before him. He decided to join in the attempt to get control of the Minnesota road and its land grant, and the famous group was complete.

George Stephen, later Baron Mount Stephen, was born in Dufftown, Banffshire, Scotland. He joined with his cousin, Donald Smith, as an investor with Hill in the St. Paul, Minneapolis & Manitoba. He also was associated with Smith as a major player in the Canadian Pacific Railway. *Author collection*

Once George Stephen had made up his mind, little time was lost. He sailed for Europe and interviewed the Amsterdam committee who was in charge of the bondholders' interest. The Dutch committee had despaired of ever seeing their money again and were wary of being assured by the receiver for funds to keep the road together. However, Stephen left Amsterdam with an option in his pocket, given for the sum of one guilder, agreeing to sell him the Dutch bonds for a sum equal to the unpaid interest, and further agreeing to wait until six months after reorganization for part of the payment.

The next step was to provide the cash required for immediate necessities. About $300,000 was put up by the members of the group. Smith arranged for an additional loan from the Bank of Montreal. This amounted to $280,000 in the first advance, and under $700,000 in all, as Stephen stated to shareholders at the bank's annual meeting in 1880. Money was advanced to the receiver to complete the most necessary extensions that were required to save the land grant, including those necessary to reach the border and join the Canadian government road being built south from Winnipeg.

The dynamic William Cornelius Van Horne was the major American-born participant in the development of the Canadian Pacific Railway and in Hill's Minnesota operations. He became a Canadian citizen, was knighted in 1894, and served as chairman of the board of the Canadian Pacific from 1899 to 1915. *Author collection*

The threatened forfeiture of the land grant was thus averted for a time. The bonds were purchased for $6.7 million, the floating obligations and part of the stock were bought up, and the mortgage, which secured the bonds, was foreclosed upon. The assets were then bought by the St. Paul, Minneapolis & Manitoba Railway Company, the new company organized for that purpose. George Stephen was president, R. B. Angus was vice president, and James Jerome Hill was general manager.

On May 23, 1879, the whole system, the successor to the dissolved St. Paul & Pacific Railroad, comprised 667 miles of right of way, of which 565 were completed; the land grant was 2.5 million acres.

Hill's early judgment of the prospective earnings of the railroad, if rehabilitated and properly managed, was thoroughly vindicated by the time he became president in 1882. That year, despite large expenditures for improvements, a 7 percent dividend was paid to stockholders. For half a century thereafter, until the depression year of 1933, the company and its successors maintained an uninterrupted record of dividend payments.

Under Hill's guiding hand, the expansion of the St. Paul, Minneapolis & Manitoba Railway in Minnesota and into Dakota Territory continued at a steady pace. By the end of 1885, the system of main and branch lines had grown to 1,470 miles.

It has been said of other sections of the American West that they were settled from the ox cart or covered wagon, while "Hill country" was settled from the boxcar. Hill laid his rails first, and then labored tirelessly to create traffic for his trains. The success of his plans for rapid expansion depended upon quick and sound colonization. Having sold his country, it was up to him to make it prosper after the settlers moved in, so he showed the farmers how to improve their methods, and in the process, became an authority on agriculture and livestock.

Hill was an early ecologist and an advocate of diversification and conservation of natural resources. He imported purebred livestock, introduced improved strains of seed, established experimental farms and credit facilities for producers, and held rates at a level that enabled settlers to sell their products competitively in distant markets. This formula enabled Hill and his associates to expand their mileage rapidly without land grants or government subsidies of any kind, other than the limited original grant of the Minnesota & Pacific.

The *Wm. Crooks* pulls a St. Paul, Minneapolis & Manitoba Railway passenger train across the 2,100-foot Stone Arch Bridge that was built between January 1862 and November 1863 to connect St. Paul to Hill's new railroad station in downtown Minneapolis. *Author collection*

In this photograph of a St. Paul, Minneapolis & Manitoba Railway dormitory car on the Northern Plains during the 1887 construction year, we see some of the U.S. Army troopers who were assigned to protect the construction teams from an American Indian attack. The iron rails cut across the land where people such as the Assiniboin and Blackfeet had lived for more than a century. *Author collection*

Meanwhile, in 1881, Hill acquired the Minneapolis & St. Cloud Railway for $30,000. Chartered in 1856, the Minneapolis & St. Cloud existed only on paper. In 25 years it had built no track, yet it held very broad rights to land grants, an asset that Hill brought into play eight years later.

In 1886 the main line of the St. Paul, Minneapolis & Manitoba was extended westward from Devil's Lake to Minot in Dakota Territory. This set the scene for one of the great epochs of railroad construction. Between April and mid-October 1887, 545 continuous miles of line, reaching across largely unsettled wilderness all the way from Minot to Great Falls in Montana Territory, was graded, bridged, and laid with track.

The logistics of an operation so distant from sources of supply were staggering, with 8,000 men and 3,300 draft horse teams pushing the construction. In one record-setting day, August 11, 1887, 44,100 feet of track was laid.

By November 18, another 97 miles were completed between Great Falls and Helena by the subsidiary Montana Central Railway Company that Hill had created in 1886, which brought the season's total to 642 miles. At Helena, the new line connected with the Northern Pacific, which had been completed to the Pacific Northwest four years earlier.

It was now time for Hill to utilize the assets of the Minneapolis & St. Cloud Railway. The obscure company existed in neither Minneapolis nor St. Cloud, but it did exist on a very important document in Hill's desk drawer.

In this nineteenth-century publicity photograph, the *Wm. Crooks* and a St. Paul, Minneapolis & Manitoba Railway passenger train are posed with the forms of transportation that preceded the iron horse on the byways of the Great Plains. On the right is a Plains Indian travois, and in the center are a two-wheeled oxcart and a stagecoach with a four-horse team. *Author collection*

Two

The Great Northern Railway

One of the greatest railroads in American history began ignominiously as a "paper" company. Although it hadn't built a mile of track in its 25 years of existence, Hill saw its potential. In 1881, he had paid the then-substantial sum of $30,000 for this virtually nonexistent and certainly anonymous Minneapolis & St. Cloud Railway because it had a very substantial asset. It had greater federal land grants than his St. Paul, Minneapolis & Manitoba Railway.

On September 18, 1889, Hill formally changed the name of the Minneapolis & St. Cloud to the Great Northern Railway Company. On February 1, 1890, the new Great Northern took over the properties of the St. Paul, Minneapolis & Manitoba. The Empire Builder now had the instrument by which he would build his empire all the way to the Pacific.

By 1890, when the Great Northern formally absorbed the St. Paul, Minneapolis & Manitoba, trackage and service ran all the way from the head of the Mississippi to the fabulously rich mines of Montana. The new railroad would be inextricably linked with Montana for the better part of the next century. Coincidently, Montana had become the 41st state in November 1889, less than two months after the Great Northern was formally created.

The route to the Pacific lay ahead in Hill's plans for the his new railroad. In order to get there, the Great Northern would have to surmount the Montana Rockies. His detractors referred to his plans of pushing the Great Northern to the Pacific as "Hill's Folly." Fortunately, Hill had an ace in the hole—John Frank Stevens.

A surveyor and engineer who later played a primary role in building the Panama Canal, Stevens had been hired to determine an easy, low altitude route

Aided by powerful steam shovels, construction crews create the right-of-way for the Great Northern Railway one mile east of Marias Pass on the segment of the mainline between Midvale and Essex, Montana. This section followed the periphery of what became Glacier National Park. *Courtesy of W. J. Yenne*

over the Rocky Mountains. On December 11, 1889, less than three months after the formal creation of the railroad, Stevens found Marias Pass, located at the headwaters of the Marias River in Montana. Not only was it an easy crossing over the Rockies, it was the easiest that existed in Montana.

The mouth of the Marias River, where it joins the Missouri River near Loma, Montana, was discovered by the Lewis and Clark expedition in June 1805. Meriwether Lewis named it Maria's River for his cousin Maria Wood. Through the years, the apostrophe was dropped, and it became the "Marias," a three-syllable word ending in "us."

This heroic statue of John Frank Stevens stands atop Marias Pass in Montana, within a few feet of the route that Stevens took when he discovered the pass on December 11, 1889. Born in 1853, the Maine native became chief engineer for the Great Northern in 1895 and spearheaded the construction of the Cascade Tunnel between 1897 and 1900. In 1905, Secretary of War William Howard Taft appointed Stevens as chief engineer of the Isthmian Canal Commission; Stevens saved the troubled project and championed the Panama Canal's lock-style design. His successor, General G. W. Goethals said, "The Canal is his (Stevens') monument." Stevens later worked with Hill to build the Spokane, Portland & Seattle Railway. The Great Northern erected the Marias Pass statue in 1925, 18 years before Stevens died. *Bill Yenne*

Lewis and William Clark debated whether to follow this river rather than the Missouri. They chose the true Missouri, which had now turned in a southerly direction. However, the Marias would have taken them to one of the easiest crossings over the Continental Divide. At its headwaters near what is now Marias Pass, they could have walked a short distance to the Middle Fork of the Flathead River near the town where the author grew up. Once on the Flathead River, they would have discovered the lake of the same name, which is the largest freshwater lake in the United States west of the Great Lakes. Lewis and Clark would have had been on easily navigable waters all the way to the Columbia, although they would have reached it much farther north than they actually did. They would also have been spared the Great Falls of the Missouri, one of their greatest obstacles. Instead, Marias Pass remained undiscovered—except by the Indians who had been using it for centuries—for 84 years.

John Stevens followed the Marias River because of what he had heard in the Indian legends, but it was the middle of the winter in the Rockies and traveling was difficult. He kept hiking into the mountains—even after his Indian guide left him—and, in his words, "walked right into the pass." The snow was too deep for him to build a fire, so to keep from freezing to death he had to tramp back and forth until morning.

Located 5,213 feet above sea level, Marias Pass was the highest point on the Great Northern Railway's transcontinental line, although it is one of the easiest crossings possible through the Rockies. The fact that the railroad had such a shallow crossing of the continent's biggest barrier was an advantage. Lewis and Clark's loss was Hill's gain.

Construction of the Great Northern's Pacific Coast extension began in April 1890 at Pacific Junction, four miles west of Havre, Montana. Between there and Puget Sound lay 815 miles of mostly wild and rugged mountain land. Except for the town of Spokane, it was virtually uninhabited. For 430 miles, the route ran through heavy timber and the sawtooth ridges of western Montana and the Idaho panhandle. Across the high desert plateau of central Washington State, the Great Northern faced another mountain obstacle. The Cascades, though lower than the crossing at Marias Pass, were steeper and presented the most difficult engineering challenge that Jim Hill faced in getting across the Northwest to the Pacific Ocean.

At the close of 1892, less than three years since Havre, only a seven-mile gap remained in what had only recently been derided as "Hill's Folly." Through a complex series of switchbacks, this final link connecting St. Paul with the Pacific was finally completed across what the railroad named Stevens Pass in honor of the heroic surveyor. On January 6, 1893, in the towering Cascades near the aptly named Scenic, Washington, the final spike was driven by the Empire Builder himself.

Seven years later, the Great Northern completed the Cascade Tunnel by boring 2.63 miles through the mountains. This permitted the railroad to abandon the treacherous switchbacks over Stevens Pass and reduced the maximum elevation in the Cascades from 4,059 to 3,383 feet. Because it was an asphyxiation hazard to operate steam locomotives through such a long tunnel, the Great Northern electrified this line and acquired four electric locomotives. Trains were pulled by steam

The Empire Builder on an inspection tour to the Pacific Northwest during his days at the helm of the Great Northern. Hill created the road in 1889 by renaming the Minneapolis & St. Cloud Railway and merging its substantial federal land grant with the infrastructure and rolling stock of his St. Paul, Minneapolis & Manitoba Railway. *Author collection*

Great Northern Railway crews lay steel into Whitefish, Montana. The road's mainline through this part of Montana was completed by 1893, but considerable fine tuning continued over the coming decades as the curves were straightened and the overall route was shortened. *Courtesy of W. J. Yenne*

Aside from the infrastructure required for crossing the Cascades, the Two Medicine River Bridge in Montana was the most dramatic piece of engineering done on the Great Northern in the nineteenth century. Standing a precarious 214 feet high, it wobbled noticeably in the high winds that are characteristic of the eastern slopes of the Rockies. Completed in 1892, it was located just outside Midvale and about a dozen miles east of Marias Pass. It was soon replaced by a steel structure that was still used in the twenty-first century. *Courtesy of W. J. Yenne*

motive power from both ends of the line and the engines switched out for the tunnel segment. Built by General Electric and the American Locomotive Company (Alco), these four-axle B-B–type units each delivered 1,000 horsepower. Unlike later electric locomotives operated by the railroad, they were not assigned a Great Northern class number.

In 1896, the Great Northern became the first American railroad to serve Japan when Jim Hill negotiated an agreement with Nippon Yusen Kaisha (NYK), the largest steamship line in the Pacific at that time. This established service between Seattle and Asian ports. It was a bold challenge to the established commerce between Europe and Asia, and marked the beginning of Seattle's status as a world port. NYK and Great Northern established rates that soon enabled them to gather up steel rails from Pittsburgh, flour from Minneapolis, and cotton from the South for shipment to Asia.

Back home, Hill was involved in an ambitious building program in St. Paul. He commissioned the firm of Peabody, Stearns, and Furber to design his palatial new home on Summit Avenue, and architect James Brodie designed the massive Great Northern office building on Third Street (now Kellogg Boulevard) that

Completed in 1892, the complex set of switchbacks that took the Great Northern across the Cascades involved an immensely complex engineering problem and an equally difficult construction problem. At least there was no shortage of timber to build the trestles. The passenger train seen here has motive power at both ends. This was necessary to get trains across the 4,059-foot Stevens Pass. *Author collection*

Great Northern Railway personnel, including several locomotive crews, pose with an early switch engine in this photograph from perhaps the late 1890s. *Courtesy of W. J. Yenne*

With two locomotives belching steam, the Great Northern *Oriental Limited* approaches Horseshoe Tunnel, near Martin Creek, in the Cascades. This was part of the slow, twisting crossing of the Cascades on the Great Northern transcontinental until the first Cascade Tunnel was completed in 1900. *Author collection*

overlooks the Mississippi River. Both are considered extraordinary examples of Richardsonian Romanesque design. This was a form that was popular with late nineteenth century captains of industry because the structures looked like European castles.

Although the Great Northern service from the Twin Cities to Puget Sound was a crowning achievement for Hill, his was not the first transcontinental railroad, nor the first across the northern tier of the United States. The former was accomplished by the Union Pacific and the Central Pacific. The latter distinction belonged to the Northern Pacific Railroad, a company that Jim Hill coveted for most of his life in the railroad industry.

The long discussed notion of spanning the continent with rails was officially sanctioned in 1862, when President Abraham Lincoln signed the Pacific Railroad Act. This coordinated the efforts of the Central Pacific, which was building east from Sacramento, and the Union Pacific, which was building westward from Omaha. These two roads crossed the nation's midsection to meet at Promontory, Utah, in May 1869 and changed the course of American history.

Henry Villard, seated in center with hat and cane, was a journalist turned railroad executive who controlled the Northern Pacific. Born Ferdinand Heinrich Gustav Hilgard in Bavaria, he emigrated in 1853, became a newspaper man, and later was a frontman for European financial interests speculating in American railroads. Under Villard's leadership, the Northern Pacific became a transcontinental railroad in 1883, but he was ousted as president in 1884. *Author collection*

Edward Henry Harriman was a dealmaker turned railroad executive who controlled both the Union Pacific and the Southern Pacific at the turn of the century. He became chairman of the Union Pacific executive committee in 1898, and he was the road's omnipotent president from 1903 until his death in 1909. He sought unsuccessfully to outmaneuver Jim Hill. *Author collection*

In 1864, President Lincoln had authorized the charter of the Northern Pacific Railroad, a transcontinental road across the northern tier of the country from Lake Superior to Puget Sound. Congress and the president were concerned with opening the Northwest to settlement and, because the Civil War was in progress, with assuring military security in the West. The war was long over when ground was finally broken for the Northern Pacific Railway on February 15, 1870, near the present town of Carlton, Minnesota, about 20 miles west of Duluth. Shortly thereafter, construction began between Tacoma and Kalama in Washington Territory. Financing shenanigans, mismanagement, the Great Panic of 1873, and bankruptcy delayed the progress of the Northern Pacific Railway for more than a decade. Henry Villard, an important nineteenth century industrialist, took over the presidency of the company in 1881, and secured overseas financing to complete the languishing road.

The Northern Pacific Railroad was completed on September 8, 1883, at Gold Creek, Montana, with the ceremonial "last spike" driven by Villard and former United States President Ulysses S. Grant. It was not a gold

Completed in 1891 on Summit Avenue in St. Paul, James Jerome Hill's massive home was designed by the firm of Peabody, Stearns, and Furber. Befitting the Empire Builder, the 36,000-square-foot palace was the largest home in Minnesota. *Minnesota Department of Tourism*

Library of Congress

spike, but it was the same steel spike used 13 years earlier to mark the beginning of construction near Carlton, Minnesota.

When the Great Panic of 1893 swept a quarter of the nation's railroad mileage into receivership, Hill made a move to unify the operations of the Great Northern and the Northern Pacific. But a plan for the Great Northern to guarantee both the principal and interest on bonds of the reorganized Northern Pacific was found by the Supreme Court to conflict with a Minnesota statute prohibiting consolidation of parallel and competing lines. The Empire Builder would not give up. Hill saw to it that the fortunes of the two roads were closely linked for the remainder of his life, although the Great Northern and the Northern Pacific Railway were not merged under the same ownership until 50 years after his death.

The Empire Builder had reached out to the Pacific and linked the headwaters of the Mississippi with the Pacific Ocean and Asia. Now Hill eyed the heart of the American heartland—the great rail hub at Chicago. Hill abhorred an empty boxcar, but the normal movement of freight over his newly completed Pacific Coast extension was certain to be predominantly westbound. To avoid the waste of hauling empty cars eastbound, and to develop the lumber industry in his territory, he drastically reduced lumber rates and opened new markets in the Mississippi and Ohio river valleys to Pacific Northwest mills.

The dominant player in the great rail hub at that time was the powerful Union Pacific Railroad, though smaller roads also had a piece of the lucrative action. One such road, the Chicago, Burlington & Quincy Railroad, was vulnerable for a takeover. The Union Pacific also had eyes for this takeover target, but they were

Library of Congress

This is the grand staircase in the James Jerome Hill Mansion in St. Paul. There were 16 crystal chandeliers such as these illuminating the 100-foot reception hall. When it opened it was one of the largest homes ever constructed with built-in electrical wiring. The carved woodwork is both oak and mahogany. *Minnesota Department of Tourism*

out-maneuvered. In 1901, the Empire Builder joined forces with his coveted Northern Pacific Railway to assume control of this road. With the support of J. P. Morgan, Hill was able to move for the joint purchase by the Great Northern and the Northern Pacific of nearly all of the outstanding stock of the Chicago, Burlington & Quincy. This alliance assured that for its entire life as a Great Northern train, the future *Empire Builder* streamliner would be able to make the run between Chicago and St. Paul on Burlington rails.

The Chicago, Burlington & Quincy acquisition gave the new parent lines access not only to Chicago, but to the markets of the Midwest and South as well. Hill became a direct competitor with the powerful Union Pacific Railroad. The Union Pacific was controlled at that time by Edward H. Harriman, a mighty railroad baron who controlled the Illinois Central Railroad, another Chicago-based road.

"Well, the 'Q' is ours," Hill said, using the popular name for the Chicago, Burlington & Quincy. "We've headed off the Union Pacific. At the same time,

The five-story, red stone James Jerome Hill Mansion boasted 13 bathrooms, 22 fireplaces, and a two-story skylit art gallery. The total construction cost in current dollars was just short of $19 million, but this included furnishings and landscaping for the adjoining three-acre estate. *Minnesota Department of Tourism*

Today, the James Jerome Hill Mansion on Summit Avenue in St. Paul is open to guided tours four days a week. The Hill family occupied the home for three decades. Mary Hill, the Empire Builder's wife, took personal charge of running the house and managing the staff until her death in 1921. *Minnesota Department of Tourism*

we've made sure we can take care of the Oriental trade. We have to look not only to cotton, but to anything that will furnish us business going to the West. We had to have access to the main centers. Out here it is a case of getting fuel or freezing."

Hill and Morgan had gone about it in a different way from the Union Pacific interests. They dealt directly with the executive committee of the Chicago, Burlington & Quincy. The railroad's shares, which had a market value of $175 to $180, were in the hands of 15,000 stockholders; the only way a successful transaction could be made was obvious. They made an offer of $200 a share, which was accepted. The Chicago, Burlington & Quincy shareholders received a good bargain, measured by the 20 to 25 point profit they were given, and the two purchasing companies received something of immense value to themselves and were capable of returning a profit at the same time, even on the new capitalization. The stock of the reorganized company was to be $100 million, divided equally between the Great Northern and the Northern Pacific.

Meanwhile, Harriman was not out of the picture. Like a master moving on a chessboard, he sought to undermine the Empire Builder by going on a buying

King Street Station in Seattle was completed in 1906, and its 245-foot Venetian-style clock tower was patterned after the sixteenth century campanile on the Piazza de San Marco in Venice, Italy. Ironically, the campanile in Venice collapsed in 1902, the year that plans for the King Street Station were first drafted; it was rebuilt to match its sixteenth century appearance, but this project was not completed until six years after the King Street Station! *Bill Yenne*

spree of Northern Pacific Railway stock. Newspapers pictured the Wall Street frenzy as a clash of titans. When the dust settled, the Empire Builder had won. A holding company incorporated under the name "Northern Securities Company" took in all Great Northern and Northern Pacific stockholders who wished to be included. Although the U.S. Supreme Court ruled against this alleged monopoly in 1904, the Empire Builder was never again challenged on his own turf.

At the turn of the twentieth century, the Great Northern had more than 5,000 miles in service with revenue per freight train mile at $3.38, which was greater than any other major railroad system in the country. Meanwhile, the average rate charged per ton mile was 20 percent less than the competing railroads in the West, a result of the Empire Builder efficiently consolidating freight into big trains and keeping the cost of operation low by avoiding "empties."

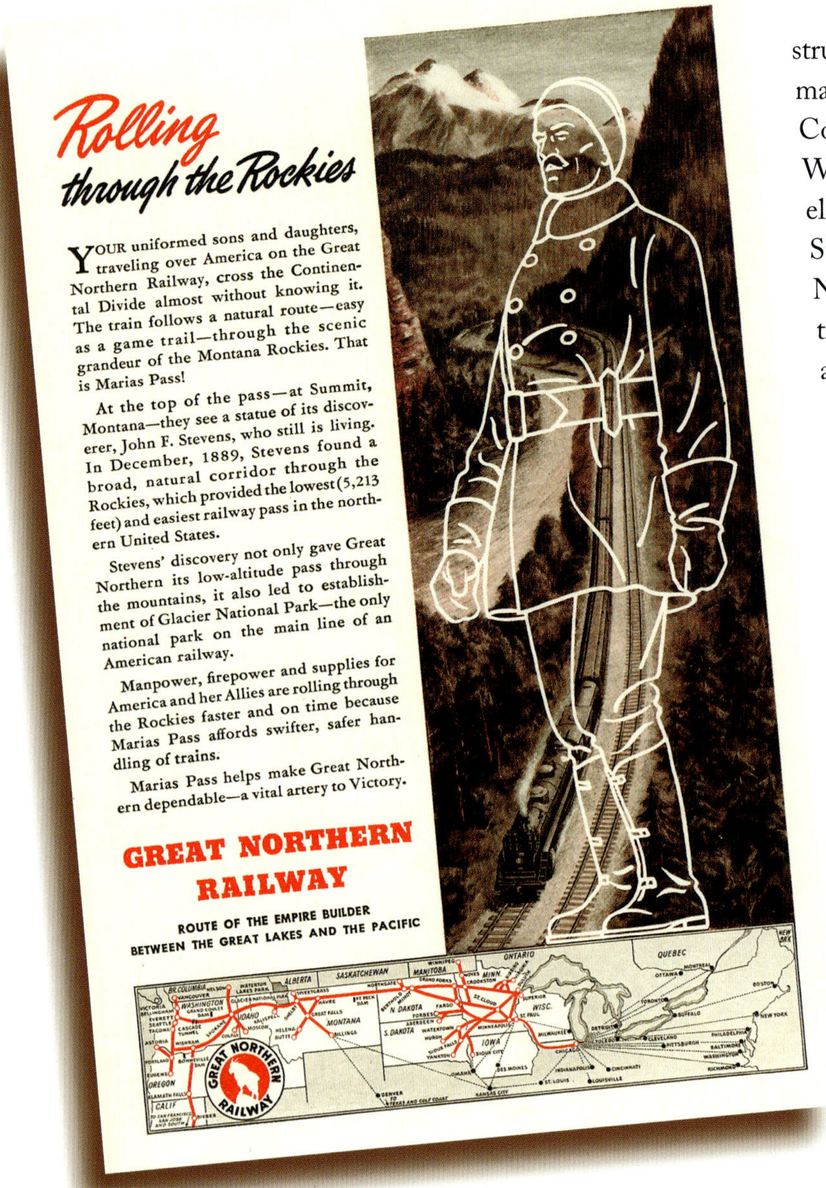

This 1943 Great Northern advertisement pays tribute to John Stevens and includes an illustration of the *Empire Builder* westbound over Marias Pass. The copy mentions that Stevens was still alive, but he passed away a few months later. *Author collection*

Jim Hill was constantly improving infrastructure. In 1904, a 69-mile relocation of the main line in Montana was completed between Columbia Falls and Rexford by way of Whitefish. In 1909, the Cascade Tunnel was electrified. In 1912, the completion of the Surrey cutoff between Fargo and Surrey, North Dakota, reduced the Great Northern's transcontinental route by 52 miles, or about an hour of through-train time.

In 1893, the Great Northern had given Seattle the railroad service it had been yearning for since 1883, when the Northern Pacific completed its transcontinental service to Tacoma, Seattle's rival Puget Sound city. In 1902, against the backdrop of Hill's efforts to merge the two lines, the Great Northern and the Northern Pacific agreed to join forces on a 5,245-foot railroad tunnel beneath downtown Seattle and build a grand station in the heart of what was then the city's central business district. The King Street Station opened in 1906.

In 1905, under Hill's aegis, the Great Northern and Northern Pacific jointly formed the Spokane, Portland & Seattle Railway Company, which built a line from Spokane, Washington, to Portland, Oregon, and subsequently acquired other lines in Oregon by purchase, lease, and building. This added new markets and sources of freight for the two Northerns. Both of the Northerns used the trackage of the Spokane, Portland & Seattle.

In 1911, the Empire Builder himself travelled to Bend, Oregon, to drive the golden spike to complete the Oregon Trunk Railway, which eventually gave the Great Northern access to northern California. This, however, did not come to pass until November 1931, through a connection with the Western Pacific Railroad at the remote Pit River Valley town of Bieber, California, 92 miles south of the Oregon border.

James Jerome Hill was a true renaissance man who was a patron of art and literature. In the 1880s and 1890s, he found time to explore the development of American exports to Asia through western ports, and the railroad transportation that could serve it. He developed the Great Northern Pacific Steamship Company to expedite such commerce, and for a while, the exportation of American raw materials and steel flourished on the West Coast.

In 1915, the same year that the Great Northern Pacific Steamship Company began service to San Francisco, the State of Minnesota named him its "greatest living citizen" at the Panama-Pacific Exposition in San Francisco.

A year later, Hill became ill and was ordered to bed by his doctor on May 17. Twelve days later, the Empire Builder was dead.

Throughout his years of creating, encouraging, and directing, Hill's creed was to develop the resources of the region the railway served. He knew the railway could not prosper unless its territory prospered. That concept and objective guided Great Northern throughout its entire history.

There is possibly no other single human being who did more to affect American railroad development than James Jerome Hill. At the time of his retirement, the region that depended upon his rails as its lifeline to the world was larger than Britain, France, and Germany combined. The Empire Builder had created a domain that exceeded, in both scope and riches, those of all except a handful of the world's potentates.

The heir apparent to the Empire Builder was his son, Louis Warren Hill. Louis succeeded him as president of the Great Northern in 1907 at the age of 35, and later became the chairman of the board. The younger Hill was a reluctant heir. He was more interested in promoting, rather than running, the railroad.

GREAT NORTHERN RAILWAY
BETWEEN GREAT LAKES AND PACIFIC

Route of the Empire Builder

TRUE STORY: GREAT NORTHERN NEVER WILL DRIVE "LAST SPIKE"

Continual Improvements of Line, Equipment and Operations Mark Railway's Progressiveness

On January 6, 1893, Great Northern became a transcontinental railway when a line extending eastward from Puget Sound was joined in the Cascade mountains with track pushed westward from the Great Lakes.

The construction crews posed that wintry day for the traditional "last spike" picture. But, actually the job of building and improving Great Northern never has stopped—in good times and bad!

Great Northern constantly has been improving its roadbed and structures by reducing grades and curves, laying heavier rail, building stronger bridges, boring time-saving tunnels, including the 8-mile Cascade Tunnel, longest in the Western Hemisphere.

Typical of the railway's forward-looking policy is the major track relocation project now under way on Great Northern's main line through the Flathead River canyon, bordering Glacier National Park in the Montana Rockies. Here three tunnels are being blasted through solid rock to eliminate several sharp curves.

A real "last spike" has not been driven on Great Northern —and never will be!

New, heavier rails and tie plates are spiked to chemically treated ties. Maintenance crews give daily attention to roadbed.

West portal of one of three new tunnels through solid rock on G. N. main line in the Montana Rockies to expedite train movements.

Steel rails are lifted by crane from G. N. flatcars and placed in position.

"Last spike" picture, taken January 6, 1893, when crews spiked rails together, joining G. N. tracks from the Great Lakes with those from Puget Sound.

The photo in the lower right of this 1945 Great Northern advertisement shows the completion of the Great Northern transcontinental mainline on January 6, 1893. The long-used Great Northern advertising theme is that the "last spike" on the road would never be driven because the Great Northern was constantly renewing itself. In fact, the Great Northern finally saw the driving of its last spike when it faded into history a quarter-century after this ad appeared. *Author collection*

Although the Great Northern delayed its last spike, there were any number of gold spikes associated with the road and its founder. Here we see an elderly James Hill on October 5, 1911, driving the gold spike at Bend, Oregon, that completed the subsidiary Oregon Trunk Railway. Through the use of this line, the Great Northern finally extended its lines into California, although that didn't happen until 1931. *Author collection*

On October 5, 1911, Ruby Faye Preddy and her mother, Mattie Preddy, rode the first train from Bend, Oregon, to Portland to celebrate Ruby's 11th birthday. Ruby is seen in the adjacent picture to the immediate right of Mr. Hill. Her mother had shouted to the crowd: "Let the little girl up front so she can see!" The crowd obliged. In this photo she is seen with her son, Jack P. Forbess, celebrating a later birthday. *Courtesy of Jack P. Forbess*

In 1919, while Louis diverted his attention to publicizing the Great Northern's interests in Glacier National Park and its evolving passenger service, Ralph Budd took the presidential reins of the Great Northern. A protege of the Empire Builder, the doe-eyed Budd had the ideal temperament to guide the road through the roaring 1920s.

One of the world's greatest engineering achievements of the 1920s was the Great Northern's new Cascade Tunnel project. Announced on Thanksgiving Day 1925 and completed in January 1929, the project included boring an all-new 7.79-mile tunnel; relocating all but seven miles of the 50-mile line between Peshastin and Scenic, Washington; eliminating 12 miles of short tunnels and snowsheds; and the electrification of 75 miles of track between Wenatchee and Skykomish, Washington.

The total cost of this historic project was approximately $25 million, and its completion was announced in a nationwide radio broadcast involving President Herbert Hoover. Still in use in the twenty-first century, the Cascade Tunnel is the longest railroad tunnel in the Western hemisphere. The second longest is the seven-mile Flathead Tunnel in northwestern Montana, which was started by the Great Northern in 1966, and completed by the Burlington Northern in 1970.

More than anything else, the impact of the Cascade Tunnel upon rail transportation was that it opened the door for the legendary *Empire Builder* to begin service five months after it formally opened.

PRESIDENTS OF THE GREAT NORTHERN

James Jerome Hill	(1889–1907)
Louis Warren Hill	(1907–1912; 1914–1919)
Carl R. Gray	(1912–1914)
Ralph Budd	(1919–1931)
William P. Kenney	(1932–1939)
Frank J. Gavin	(1939–1951)
John M. Budd	(1951–1970)

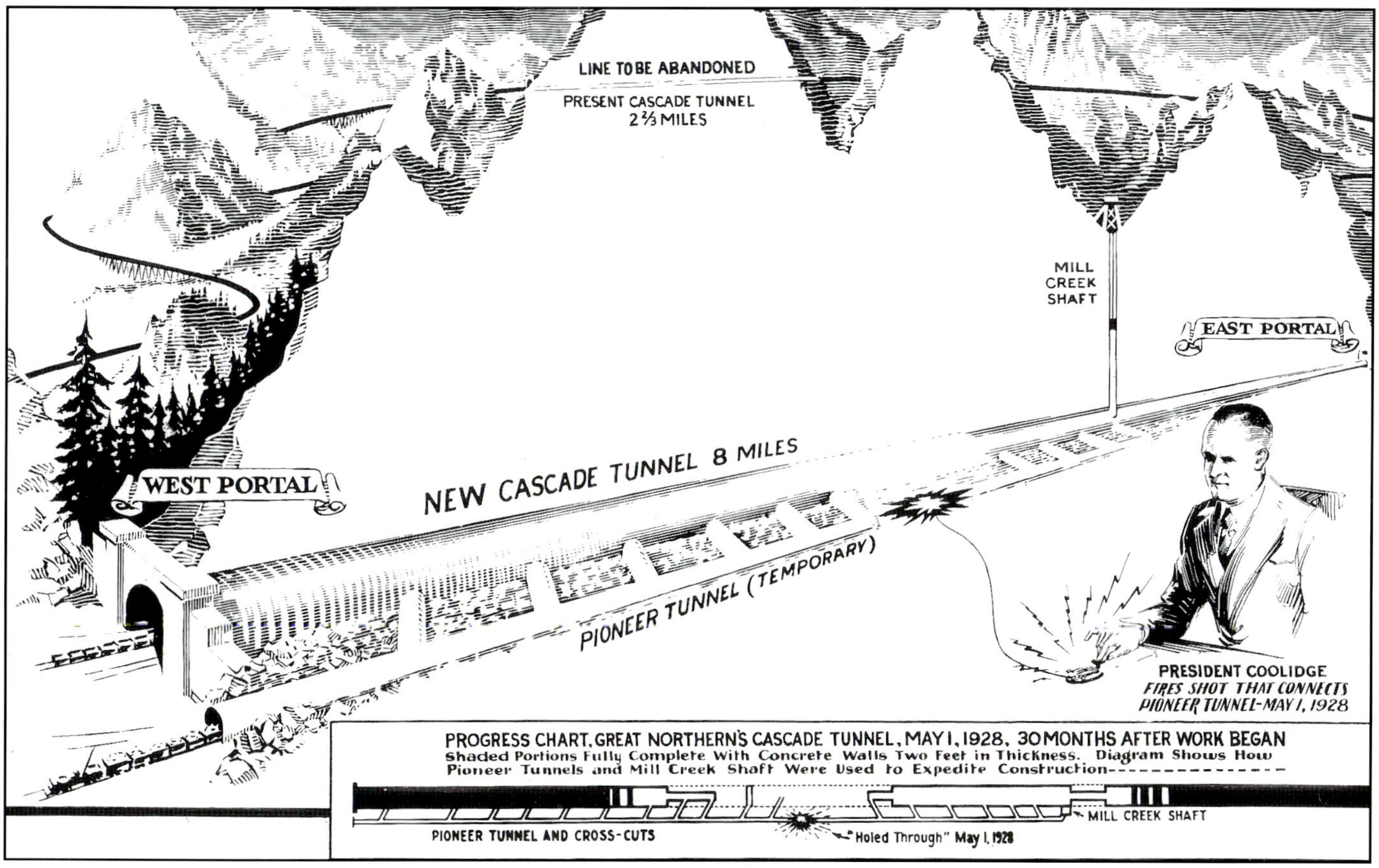

The crowning engineering achievement on the Great Northern prior to the inauguration of the *Empire Builder* was the New Cascade Tunnel. Drilling began from both ends late in 1925. This illustration shows President Calvin Coolidge firing the dynamite shot that connected the two ends on May 1, 1928. He sat in the White House and sent the electric spark that ignited the blasting cap with a telegraph key. This was all very high-tech for the era. The tunnel wasn't open for service for another eight months after this photo was taken. In this cutaway drawing, the length was billed as eight miles, but it was actually 7.79 miles. *Author collection*

Three

Launching the *Empire Builder*

The golden age of American passenger rail travel, the 1920s to the 1950s, was characterized as much by marketing as by motive power and rolling stock. All of the great railroads had their signature streamliners. The New York Central had its *20th Century Limited*, while the rival Pennsylvania Railroad had its *Broadway Limited*. The Wabash had its *Cannonball*, the Burlington its *Zephyrs*, and the Illinois Central had its storied *City of New Orleans*. Out west, there was the legendary *Daylight* on the Southern Pacific and the family of *Chiefs* on the Atchison, Topeka & Santa Fe. For the Great Northern Railway, the signature streamliner bore the nickname of the founder—the *Empire Builder*.

It has been said that deluxe passenger service was not a priority for the namesake of the *Empire Builder*, but that was only partially true. James Jerome Hill was a businessman, and in the pie chart of income from railroad operations, freight business accounted for 80 percent. Hill had not ignored the passenger side of the business, but his early years on this side was characterized by his interest in low-cost transportation to bring settlers into the areas of North Dakota and Montana where they would homestead, farm, and ship produce on Great Northern freight trains. By the 1890s, the business had matured and Hill matured with it.

Both Jim Hill and his son Louis understood the prestige value in having a luxurious train on their route. Before the *Empire Builder*, the Great Northern offered luxury passenger service from the Midwest to the Pacific Northwest for nearly four decades. Jim Hill had launched the first Great Northern passenger train across the continent on the 72-hour run from St. Paul to Seattle on June 18, 1893, just five months after the Great Northern line was completed across the Cascades. Even then, the Great Northern had spared no expense to make the transcontinental train

A 16-car Great Northern *Empire Builder* snakes its way through Kootenai Canyon between Troy, Montana, and Bonner's Ferry, Idaho. This section was scheduled for daylight so passengers could enjoy the scenery. *Author collection*

The first *Empire Builder* leaves St. Paul Union Depot for its inaugural run on June 11, 1929. The Great Northern ordered 28 of these 4-8-2 Mountain locomotives from the Baldwin Locomotive Works and operated them under the Class P-2 designation. They were standard equipment on the *Empire Builder* in its early days. *Author collection*

a deluxe affair. The dining car was appointed in polished oak, and the interior was the height of Victorian fashion with thick carpets and flamboyant gas lamps.

After a decade of service to Seattle, the Great Northern offered two daily departures on the run in 1903. In the autumn of 1905, this service was finally given a name. Hill, who relished the image of his railroad as a gateway to Asia, decided to call his Midwest to Pacific Northwest train the *Oriental Limited*. With this in mind, the interior decor was now influenced by motifs from Asian art.

Hill soon enhanced this operation and linked it to the service between Chicago and St. Paul that was offered by the Chicago, Milwaukee & St. Paul Railroad, then a non-threatening smaller player in the Chicago trade. As soon as Hill took control of the Chicago, Burlington & Quincy in 1901, that road's *Northwest Limited* service out of Denver was also linked to the Great Northern transcontinental. This

was by way of the Great Northern's Montana branch line from Billings, via Great Falls, to Shelby, where it intersected with the *Oriental Limited.* Meanwhile, the Great Northern had trackage rights on the Chicago, Burlington & Quincy between Chicago and St. Paul. The *Oriental Limited*, like the later *Empire Builder*, operated on this line through its entire history.

Aboard the *Oriental Limited*, standards of comfort and convenience were set. Interior decorators based their palette on shades of tan, which blended nicely with the rustic feel of the intermountain West. In 1908, the gas lamps aboard the *Oriental Limited* were replaced by safer and more efficient electric lighting. The club car boasted the Booklover's Library. There was a barber shop, and daily newspapers were taken aboard. A gentleman could relax with a cigar and a brandy, just as he might in his own club back home.

This early photograph of a Great Northern passenger train crossing the Mississippi River on the Stone Arch Bridge between St. Paul and Minneapolis probably shows a nine-car *Oriental Limited*. *Author collection*

In January 1914, the Empire Builder proudly opened the new Great Northern Railway Station on Hennepin Avenue in Minneapolis. Located 30 timetable minutes west of the rival St. Paul Union Depot, the facility remained in service until 1978 and was used by the Northern Pacific; Chicago Great Western; the Chicago, Burlington & Quincy; and several smaller railroads. By 1916, the Great Northern Station handled 125 trains and 5,700 passengers each day, compared to an average of 500 trains at St. Paul, then the second busiest station in the country after South Station in Boston.

Also in 1914, the Great Northern made a major investment in motive power to pull these luxury hotels on wheels. The order went out to the Baldwin Locomotive Works for 25 4-6-2 Pacific Class locomotives and 15 of the more powerful 4-8-2 Mountain Class units. In 1903, the Great Northern had instituted an in-house locomotive classification system to classify its own inventory of steam locomotives. Under this system, the 4-6-2 Pacifics were referred to as Class H, and the 4-8-2 Mountains were Great Northern Class P locomotives.

During World War I, the temporary nationalization of the American railroad industry through the U.S. Railroad Administration had thrown that industry into chaos. Attempts at standardization and deferred maintenance meant that the railroads had to spend the early 1920s playing catch-up.

At the Great Northern, both Ralph Budd and Louis Hill saw the need to dust off the road's image in the realm of passenger service. On June 1, 1924, the Great Northern relaunched the *Oriental Limited* as though it were an all-new service. In a sense, it was. The Great Northern entered into a contract with the Pullman Company to supply most of its sleeping cars and the open-topped observation cars that made travel through the spectacular Rocky Mountains in Montana more exciting. In the dining cars on the "new" *Oriental Limited*, the Great Northern sought to keep prices reasonably low. A complete dinner cost less than $2, about $20 by today's prices. Great Northern promotional materials called the *Oriental Limited* "a monument to modern railroad transportation; a train that represents the utmost in all that experienced and discriminating travelers demand."

Coal-powered locomotives were being phased out and replaced by oil-burning locomotives for passenger service. This was happening throughout the industry, but the Great Northern seized upon the fact as a marketing hook. Suddenly the phrase "Clean and Cinderless" appeared in Great Northern advertising.

Departure time was exciting on the Great Northern's new *Empire Builder*. Departures from Chicago and the Twin Cities were timed so that the *Empire Builder* crossed North Dakota in the dark and passed the Montana Rockies by day. The fast, luxurious all-steel train ran a 63-hour schedule westbound and a 61 3/4-hour schedule eastbound. *Author collection*

The Great Northern acquired 25 2-8-8-0 locomotives from the Baldwin Locomotive Works under the internal Class N-1 designation. Built between July and September 1912, they weighed 225 tons and delivered 93,250 pounds of tractive effort on 63-inch driving wheels.

Between February 1924 and April 1927, these locomotives were rebuilt at the Great Northern's Superior shop (except for one rebuilt at the Dale Street shop) to retrofit them with simple (instead of compound) cylinders and increase tractive effort by nearly 10 percent. With this retrofit, the equipment was redesignated as Class N-2. A further rebuilding effort in 1940 and 1941 resulted in the same 25 locomotives emerging as the Class N-3, with 118,400 pounds of tractive effort and an increase in boiler pressure from 210 psi to 300 psi. New nickel-steel boilers were part of the N-3 retrofit, which increased the overall weight to 286 tons.

No. 1800 was one of five 2-6-6-2 Mallet-Compound Articulated locomotives built for the Great Northern by the Baldwin Locomotive Works in 1906 during the early years of the *Oriental Limited*. She weighed 17 tons and served as a Great Northern Class L unit. *Author collection*

The new Cascade Tunnel project was completed in January 1929, and with it came the electrification of the 75 miles of track between Wenatchee and Skykomish, Washington. In anticipation of this extensive electrification effort, the Great Northern also made a major investment in electric motive power. The company bought 14 electric locomotives between December 1926 and October 1928, and had an additional four built in August 1930.

The first group were 10 Baldwin-Westinghouse 1,830 horsepower single phase 1-D-1 units, which were designated Class Z-1 by Great Northern. The next batch, including the four built in 1930, were 3,000-horsepower single-phase 1-C+C-1 units. These were manufactured by General Electric and the American Locomotive Company (Alco) and identified as Great Northern Class Y-1. All of these 18 electric locomotives were delivered in Pullman Green paint. While all but one of the Y-1 units were eventually repainted in *Empire Builder* livery, the Z-1s remained in Pullman Green until they were all withdrawn from service in August 1956.

With the Cascade Tunnel in operation at the beginning of 1929, the Great Northern was one of America's leading railroads. It had 8,368 miles of main line track and a fleet of 1,164 locomotives drawing 55,777 freight cars and 946 passenger cars. This was also the first year the Great Northern's advertising budget topped a million dollars.

In addition to the Cascade Tunnel project, the Great Northern reconfigured its entire main line with either semaphore or light-type block signals. By 1929, steel rails weighing 110 pounds to the yard were installed on straight sections of track, and 130-pounds-to-the-yard steel was used on curves. The track was heavily ballasted with washed gravel, and grades and curves were reduced to a minimum. This was done both for the safety and smooth ride required for passenger service, but also to permit faster speeds to meet new, tighter schedules for both passenger and freight service.

The next step in terms of passenger service was to inaugurate a new service that was even more classy than the recently reinvented *Oriental Limited.* In June 1929, the first month of summer after the opening the new tunnel, the Great Northern received the ultimate signature train.

The first run of the *Empire Builder* left the St. Paul Union Depot on June 10, 1929. The first stop was the Great Northern Station in Minneapolis. Since the completion of the Great Northern Station in 1914, the St. Paul Union Depot had been completely rebuilt in the monumental neoclassic style that was so much in vogue for public buildings in the roaring 1920s. With its Doric columns and Tennessee marble, it was an appropriate starting point for the Great Northern's new signature line. It was partially built on land that Jim Hill had purchased in 1903. Although the Union Depot had formally opened in April 1920, further construction work went on for most of the decade.

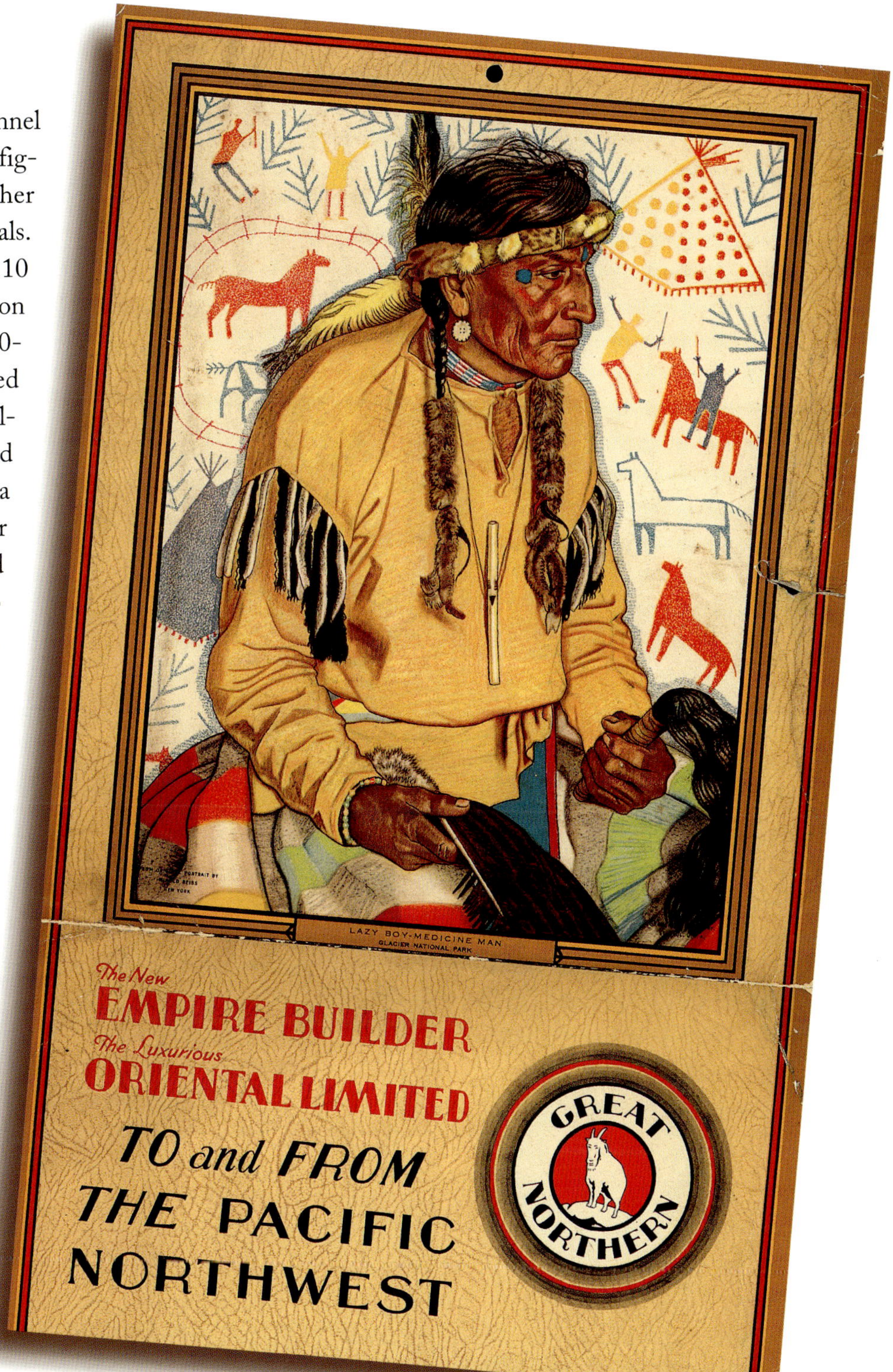

Lazy Boy, a Blackfeet man identified as a medicine man, was the subject of this Great Northern calendar illustration by Winold Reiss. Born in Karlsruhe, Germany, Reiss emigrated to the United States in 1913 and established himself in New York working as an illustrator. Louis Hill hired him to travel to Montana and do a series of Blackfeet paintings advertising the *Empire Builder* and the *Oriental Limited. Author collection*

Above: The Sun Parlor observation car boasted extra-high windows to permit "an unobstructed view of the innumerable scenic spots passed on the route of the *Empire Builder*." *Author collection*

Above right: In the *Empire Builder's* comfortable Club Lounge, patrons found "all the conveniences that they expect in their own clubs, or in the better metropolitan hotels." *Author collection*

The first run of the *Empire Builder* was pulled as far as the Cascade Tunnel by a Baldwin 4-8-2 Mountain–type locomotive, identified in Great Northern nomenclature as a Class P-2 locomotive. The *Empire Builder* was described as the "new companion train of the *Oriental Limited*. . . . A new all steel train that marks another forward step in the fulfillment of the plans of the railroad's founder, James J. Hill, and it is to honor him that the new train has taken the title Mr. Hill so richly merited—the *Empire Builder*."

Baldwin Locomotive Works built 28 of the Class P-2 units in September and October 1923. They weighed 365,600 pounds and had a tractive effort of 54,840 on eight 73-inch driving wheels. Of course, the new *Empire Builder* was cinderless, and the oil-burning locomotives were used for most of the run and electric operations through the new Cascade Tunnel. Furthermore, the efficiency of the new route using the new tunnel saved a whole business day for transcontinental travelers between Chicago and the cities of the Pacific Northwest.

The Great Northern configured six *Empire Builder* trains, which operated on a 63-hour schedule westbound from Chicago to Seattle, and a 61-hour 15-minute schedule on the eastbound return. As had been the case with the *Oriental Limited*, the *Empire Builder* ran on the rails of the Chicago, Burlington & Quincy between Chicago and St. Paul, and on Great Northern track from St. Paul to Seattle. In Spokane, the train was split, with a portion of the cars going south and west to Portland via the tracks of the Spokane, Portland & Seattle Railway, which was owned jointly by the Great Northern and Northern Pacific.

Great Northern boasted, "In fixing a time saving schedule so appealing to the busy business men and women whose duties or pleasures carry them from coast to coast, the Great Northern Railway has sacrificed nothing of the comforts, which for five years have characterized the *Oriental Limited,* and which during that time, have pleasantly and indelibly impressed themselves on the memories of its patrons. On the contrary, every device which the combined efforts of designers, builders, and operators can produce for the comfort of travelers has been added to the equipment of the *Empire Builder*."

No. 1959 was a 2-6-8-0 Mallet-Articulated locomotive delivered by the Baldwin Locomotive Works in 1910, and it operated as a Great Northern Class M unit. Frequently rebuilt through the years, the Class M locomotives remained in service until the 1950s. *Railroad Museum of Pennsylvania, H.L. Broadbelt Collection*

The Baldwin Locomotive Works began delivering the Great Northern Class N, 2-8-8-0 Mallet-Articulated units in 1912. This view of such a unit pulling a long freight through the Rockies gives us an idea of the muscle in these big locomotives. *Courtesy of W. J. Yenne*

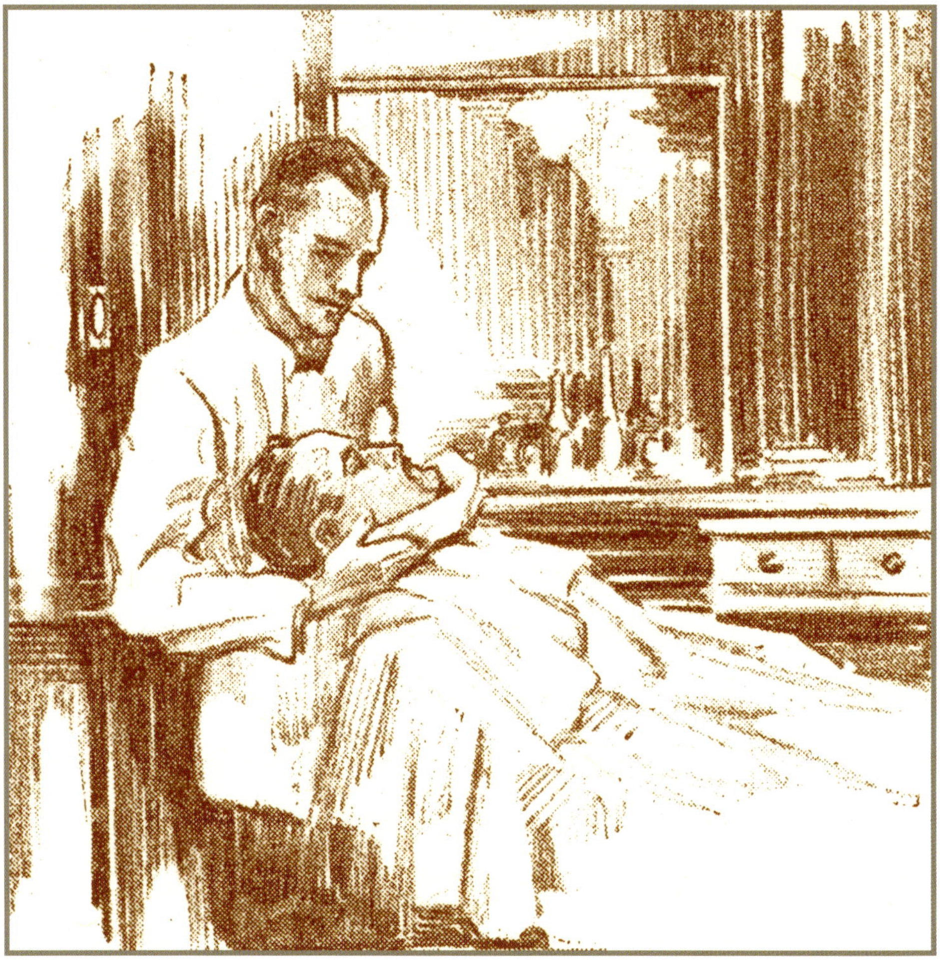

As the *Empire Builder* was originally configured, the Club Lounge car had a barber shop tucked into the forward part of the car. The Great Northern advertised reasonable prices. *Author collection*

Customer service, already a strong selling point for the *Oriental Limited*, became the guiding philosophy aboard the *Empire Builder*. "The desire of the Great Northern to serve its guests to a superlative degree of excellence has been the inspiration and aim from the start," the company explained. "Genuine hospitality is everywhere reflected in the deportment of all train attendants whose sole object is to minister as capably as they possibly can to the desires of those on board. The Great Northern justly prides itself on a personnel that takes something more than a dutiful interest in its patrons. Here, then, is unsurpassed service concentrated in a train that recognizes only one equal, and that in its companion, the *Oriental Limited*. Like the *Oriental Limited*, the *Empire Builder*, notwithstanding its many exclusive features, is not an extra fare train."

The keynote of the decorative strategy that defined the *Empire Builder* was said to have been the big 89-foot Sun Parlor observation cars. The new cars contained

A 4-8-2 Mountain unit pulls the *Empire Builder* across the Mississippi River on the Stone Arch Bridge. The Mountains served as Great Northern Class P-2. This particular P-2 was built by the Baldwin Locomotive Works in October 1923 and was scrapped in Duluth in October 1957. *Author collection*

The *Empire Builder* dining car, like that of the *Oriental Limited*, accommodated 36 people. Here we see an army officer arriving to meet his friend for dinner. The Great Northern was justifiably proud of the food that was served aboard the *Empire Builder*. *Author collection*

The engineer smiles at the camera as he prepares for an *Empire Builder* run in this Great Northern Class P-2 unit. This particular locomotive was one of 25 4-8-2 Mountain units built by the Baldwin Locomotive Works for the Great Northern in October 1923. After years of pulling the *Empire Builder* through Willmar, Minnesota, it was retired in April 1958 and donated to that city in October 1965. Today, it is preserved at the Kandiyohi County Historical Society on Highway 71 in Willmar. *Author collection*

For day use, the lower berths in the *Empire Builder's* Pullman sleeping cars folded out into seats. They were comfortable only as long as you didn't have another passenger sitting next to you. The reading lamps were all electric. *Author's collection*

the service features that were beginning to be considered necessary in transcontinental travel at the dawn of the golden age of American rail travel. At the rear of the car was the spacious Sun Parlor itself. Previously, the last car in a typical passenger train featured a recessed rear platform. The Sun Parlor was completely enclosed by glass with eight large, comfortable chairs. The windows of the parlor, like those of the adjoining observation lounge, were taller to give the passengers an unobstructed view of the marvelous scenery along the route.

The Sun Parlor also had its own compact buffet, which was run by the car porter. It offered complete fountain and broiler service for quick snacks while you were enjoying the scenery. Cigars, cigarettes, and playing cards were also available.

Double Steel and Two Cutter were Blackfeet women who posed for Winold Reiss at his studio in East Glacier, Montana. Hired by Louis Hill to create advertising art for the Great Northern, Reiss lived in Glacier most summers between 1927 and 1937, and he operated an art school between 1934 and 1937. *Author collection*

The Baldwin Locomotive Works delivered the first 30 2-10-2 locomotives to the Great Northern in 1923. They served on the main line as the Great Northern Class Q and were paired with 15,000-gallon Vanderbilt tenders. *Railroad Museum of Pennsylvania, H.L. Broadbelt Collection*

The predominant color was the same tan that was so well-liked by *Oriental Limited* passengers. However, in the Sun Parlor observation cars, colorfully upholstered settees and chairs provided a bright accent and what the company promotional literature called "a new and decidedly attractive touch to the room." Also decorated in such a manner was the Club Lounge, where passengers were invited to chat and play cards. The lighting fixtures on the *Empire Builder* were finished in antique gold. Adjacent to the upholstered furniture were small consoles and end tables with parchment-shaded electric lamps.

This "action shot" of the *Empire Builder*, circa the early 1930s, was probably taken when the train was stopped. This Baldwin Locomotive Works 4-8-4 Northern was built in April 1929 in anticipation of the inauguration of *Empire Builder* service. Serving for almost three decades as a Great Northern Class S-1 unit, it was retired in December 1957 and scrapped in 1963. *Author collection*

On the end tables, the *Empire Builder* staff laid out a selection of current magazines and descriptive literature about the history and scenic attractions of the country along the train route. Such literature was offered by the Great Northern for as long as it ran the train, and it is offered on the Amtrak *Empire Builder* in the twenty-first century.

A writing desk was situated in a quiet corner of the Sun Parlor observation cars. It was supplied with notepaper, envelopes, and mailing cards. When their letters were written, passengers could buy postage stamps from the porter, who also saw that the missives were mailed.

For more urgent communications, telegraph blanks were available at the writing desk in the Sun Parlor. There was even a telephone, which couldn't be used when the train was in motion, but when the *Empire Builder* pulled into a Great Northern station, there were terminal points where the porter could connect the patron with a land line.

Adjacent to the Club Lounge was the ladies' dressing room, which was equipped with a shower bath. At the opposite end of the lounge was the men's shower. Adjoining these areas, the Great Northern provided a manicurist and hair dresser for the ladies, and an enclosed barber shop for the men. If a passenger needed his or her clothes cleaned and pressed, they gave the clothes to the sleeping car porter at night, and it was back in the morning.

The Great Northern *Empire Builder* makes its run along the Kootenai River between Troy, Montana, and Bonner's Ferry, Idaho. It was at Troy that the *Empire Builder* conductor officially changed his big gold pocket watch from Mountain Time to Pacific Time.
Author collection

"The Route of the *Empire Builder*" bisected lands that were strange and fascinating for people in the east who were unfamiliar with them. Blackfeet people were seen by the Great Northern as an essential part of the ethos of the Mountain West where the railroad took vacationers. The Winold Reiss illustration of Riding Black Horse was painted from life in Montana and used on a series of *Empire Builder* dining car menus. *Author collection*

Having earned a reputation for quality dining cars, the Great Northern paid special attention to those on the new *Empire Builder*. As company literature of the era extolled, "Exclusive features have been introduced for the pleasure of the guests of this deluxe train. The kitchen and pantry are unusually large. All of the latest conveniences in ice boxes, lockers, and containers guarantee fresh and pure food, and automatic dish-washing machines assure cleanliness in table ware. The problem of ventilation, and therefore, the elimination of cooking odors has been completely solved. Moreover, the car is so constructed that vibration has been reduced to a minimum, another pleasant prospect for those who choose to ride on the *Empire Builder*."

The dining cars on the *Oriental Limited* had seated 36 passengers who enjoyed both *table d'hote* and *a la carte* meals. The diners in service on the *Empire Builder* matched the number of seats, while Great Northern promotional literature touted enhanced service. "With the improved methods employed in the kitchen, the service is even more pronounced in its efficiency, thereby cutting down the waiting time and adding generally to the enjoyment of the meals."

For efficiency and to ensure freshness, the Great Northern acquired produce and dairy products from the local agricultural producers along the route. This fact was used in promoting the *Empire Builder*. Along these lines, the Great Northern arranged for a specialized summer service that was more of a gimmick than efficient, but it was truly loved by *Empire Builder* passengers. At Stryker, 30 miles west of Whitefish, Montana, the Great Northern telegraph operator went trout fishing on company time. As the *Empire Builder* came through in the late afternoon, it would stop long enough to pick up his day's catch for the dining car staff, who'd prepare the freshly caught trout for the evening meal.

Operated by the Pullman Company, the sleeping cars on the *Empire Builder* were state of the art, and the Great Northern offered the "assurance of a restful trip across the middle and western part of the continent." The standard sleepers used

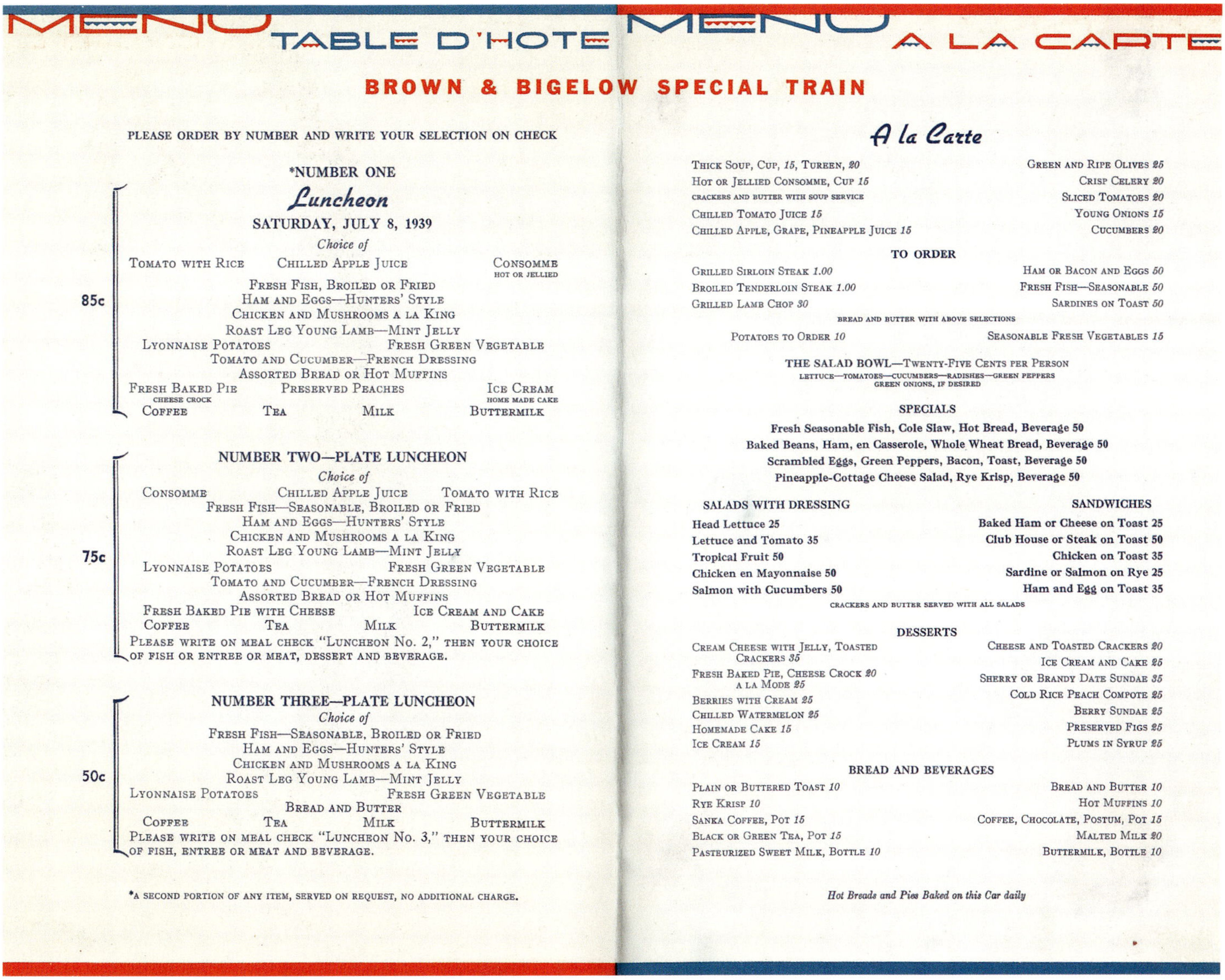

MENU TABLE D'HOTE MENU A LA CARTE

BROWN & BIGELOW SPECIAL TRAIN

PLEASE ORDER BY NUMBER AND WRITE YOUR SELECTION ON CHECK

*NUMBER ONE

Luncheon

SATURDAY, JULY 8, 1939

Choice of

85c

Tomato with Rice — Chilled Apple Juice — Consomme (hot or jellied)

Fresh Fish, Broiled or Fried
Ham and Eggs—Hunters' Style
Chicken and Mushrooms a la King
Roast Leg Young Lamb—Mint Jelly

Lyonnaise Potatoes — Fresh Green Vegetable

Tomato and Cucumber—French Dressing
Assorted Bread or Hot Muffins

Fresh Baked Pie (cheese crock) — Preserved Peaches — Ice Cream (home made cake)

Coffee — Tea — Milk — Buttermilk

NUMBER TWO—PLATE LUNCHEON

Choice of

75c

Consomme — Chilled Apple Juice — Tomato with Rice

Fresh Fish—Seasonable, Broiled or Fried
Ham and Eggs—Hunters' Style
Chicken and Mushrooms a la King
Roast Leg Young Lamb—Mint Jelly

Lyonnaise Potatoes — Fresh Green Vegetable

Tomato and Cucumber—French Dressing
Assorted Bread or Hot Muffins

Fresh Baked Pie with Cheese — Ice Cream and Cake

Coffee — Tea — Milk — Buttermilk

Please write on meal check "Luncheon No. 2," then your choice of fish or entree or meat, dessert and beverage.

NUMBER THREE—PLATE LUNCHEON

Choice of

50c

Fresh Fish—Seasonable, Broiled or Fried
Ham and Eggs—Hunters' Style
Chicken and Mushrooms a la King
Roast Leg Young Lamb—Mint Jelly

Lyonnaise Potatoes — Fresh Green Vegetable

Bread and Butter

Coffee — Tea — Milk — Buttermilk

Please write on meal check "Luncheon No. 3," then your choice of fish, entree or meat and beverage.

*A second portion of any item, served on request, no additional charge.

A la Carte

Thick Soup, Cup, 15, Tureen, 20
Hot or Jellied Consomme, Cup 15
Crackers and butter with soup service
Chilled Tomato Juice 15
Chilled Apple, Grape, Pineapple Juice 15

Green and Ripe Olives 25
Crisp Celery 20
Sliced Tomatoes 20
Young Onions 15
Cucumbers 20

TO ORDER

Grilled Sirloin Steak 1.00
Broiled Tenderloin Steak 1.00
Grilled Lamb Chop 30

Ham or Bacon and Eggs 50
Fresh Fish—Seasonable 50
Sardines on Toast 50

Bread and butter with above selections

Potatoes to Order 10 — Seasonable Fresh Vegetables 15

THE SALAD BOWL—Twenty-Five Cents per Person
Lettuce—Tomatoes—Cucumbers—Radishes—Green Peppers
Green Onions, if desired

SPECIALS

Fresh Seasonable Fish, Cole Slaw, Hot Bread, Beverage 50
Baked Beans, Ham, en Casserole, Whole Wheat Bread, Beverage 50
Scrambled Eggs, Green Peppers, Bacon, Toast, Beverage 50
Pineapple-Cottage Cheese Salad, Rye Krisp, Beverage 50

SALADS WITH DRESSING

Head Lettuce 25
Lettuce and Tomato 35
Tropical Fruit 50
Chicken en Mayonnaise 50
Salmon with Cucumbers 50

SANDWICHES

Baked Ham or Cheese on Toast 25
Club House or Steak on Toast 50
Chicken on Toast 35
Sardine or Salmon on Rye 25
Ham and Egg on Toast 35

Crackers and butter served with all salads

DESSERTS

Cream Cheese with Jelly, Toasted Crackers 35
Fresh Baked Pie, Cheese Crock 20
a la Mode 25
Berries with Cream 25
Chilled Watermelon 25
Homemade Cake 15
Ice Cream 15

Cheese and Toasted Crackers 20
Ice Cream and Cake 25
Sherry or Brandy Date Sundae 35
Cold Rice Peach Compote 25
Berry Sundae 25
Preserved Figs 25
Plums in Syrup 25

BREAD AND BEVERAGES

Plain or Buttered Toast 10
Rye Krisp 10
Sanka Coffee, Pot 15
Black or Green Tea, Pot 15
Pasteurized Sweet Milk, Bottle 10

Bread and Butter 10
Hot Muffins 10
Coffee, Chocolate, Postum, Pot 15
Malted Milk 20
Buttermilk, Bottle 10

Hot Breads and Pies Baked on this Car daily

This menu transports us back to the *Empire Builder* dining car at lunch time on Saturday, July 8, 1939. Breads and desserts were made on the train daily. To get an idea of these prices in today's dollars, divide by 0.081. The 85 cent luncheon would be $10.50 today, which is still a good deal considering that seconds were free. A pot of coffee would be $1.85, which is a better price than you can get on a single cup at the take-out place on the corner today. *Author collection*

on the *Empire Builder* during the early years contained eight sleeping sections, a drawing room, and two compartments. The private rooms were arranged so that a drawing room and compartment could be combined. A similar feature was offered as long as the Great Northern operated the train.

Described as "wide and roomy," the sleeping berths were individually lighted and ventilated, using sash ventilators so the passengers could regulate their own supply of air. In the lower berth, the head rests on the seats were adjustable and became a horizontal shelf for clothes and luggage, while the upper berths were equipped with a shelf for passengers' personal property. As early as 1929, the berths were equipped with coil-spring mattresses. Each section was shut off from "too

One of the two stops made by the *Empire Builder* in central Washington was at Wenatchee, the capital of that state's world-famous apple-producing region. The Cashmere Pioneer Growers created a bushel-sized "Fancy Special Pack" of apples and branded it with the *Empire Builder* name. *Author collection*

much public view" by a permanent headboard, which Great Northern boasted "assures guests an opportunity for seclusion that is rarely possible on a train."

Aisle lights and luminous berth numbers were installed to avoid the nagging confusion that often reigned in sleeping cars during the night as half-asleep passengers went to the bathrooms. While all of the *Empire Builder* cars were heated, air conditioning was added in 1935 to take the edge off those sweltering summer days in the upper Midwest.

The dressing rooms on the *Empire Builder* Pullman sleepers featured white porcelain fixtures, dressing tables, boudoir chairs, extra lighting facilities, and what the Great Northern bragged to be "unusually ample space [to] make dressing on the *Empire Builder* as free from jostling as it is at home."

To augment the 28 Baldwin 4-8-2 Class P-2 locomotives, the Great Northern ordered a half-dozen 4-8-4 Northern–type locomotives. Built in April and May 1929, on the eve of the inauguration of *Empire Builder* service, they operated under the Great Northern Class S-1 designation. Weighing 236 tons, they had 68,470 pounds of tractive effort, 73-inch drivers, and cylinders measuring 28 by 30 inches. In March and April 1930, the *Empire Builder* received 14 Baldwin S-2 Class 4-8-4 locomotives. They weighed 420,900 pounds, with a tractive effort of 58,310 pounds on 80-inch drivers.

When the *Empire Builder* was launched, the Great Northern boasted that "the most powerful fleet of locomotives in the world will haul this new all steel train, and for over 1,200 miles, either oil burning or electric engines are used, which means that over that stretch which pierces the most scenic sections of the Northwest, passengers are assured of clean, cinderless travel."

These words clearly cast the *Empire Builder* in a positive light as the United States was about to be side-tracked into one of its darkest hours. In October 1929, just four months after the *Empire Builder* entered service, the New York stock market crashed, and the nation began the precipitous tumble into the Great Depression.

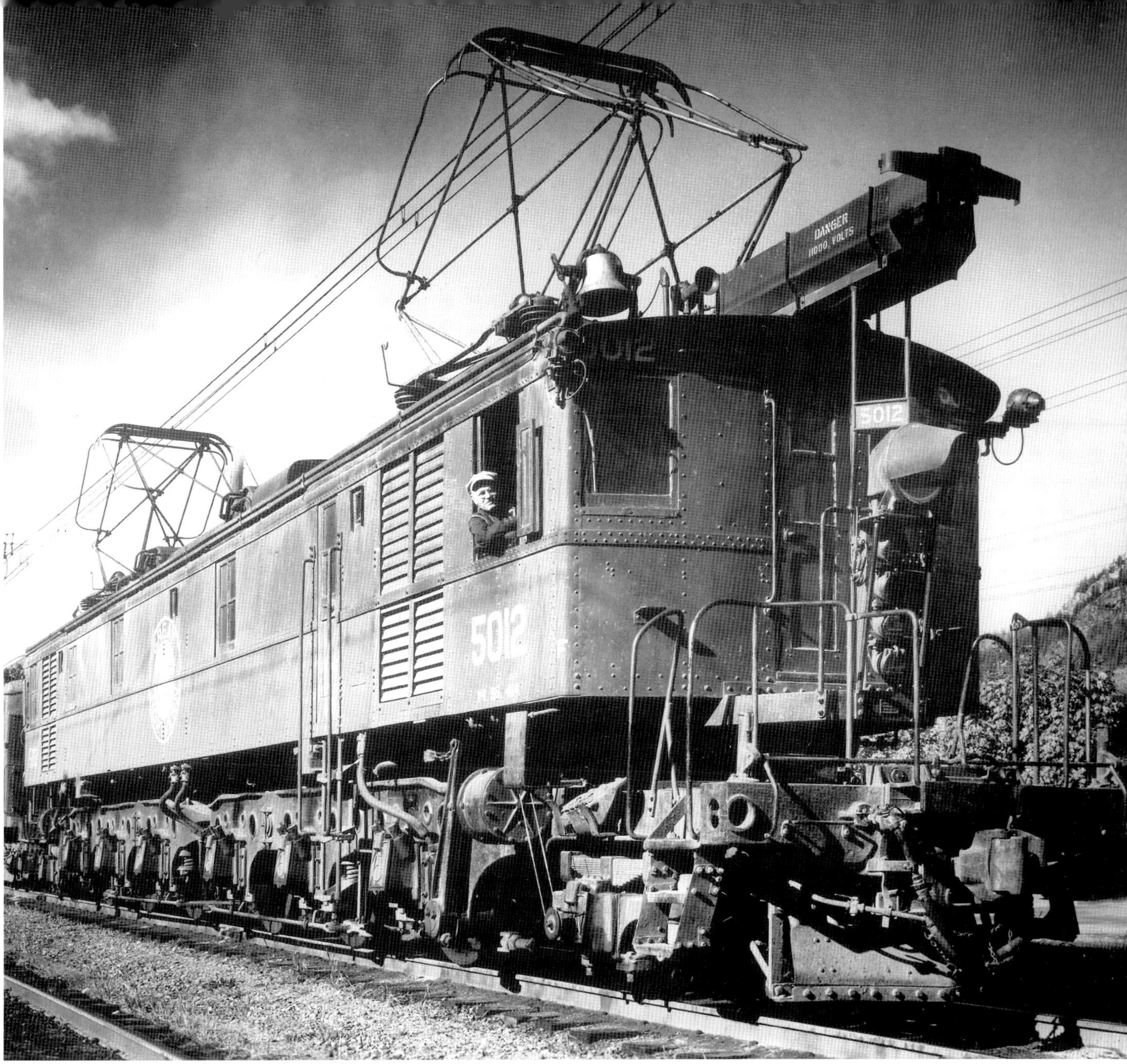

The *Empire Builder,* pulled by one of eight Y-1 electrics operated by the Great Northern, exits the Cascade Tunnel at Skykomish. This particular unit was built in September 1928 by General Electric and Alco. It served the Great Northern and the *Empire Builder* until August 1956, when the Cascade Tunnel was ventilated. It was sold to the Pennsylvania Railroad and operated in the East until 1962. *Author collection*

The crisp and effusive prose written about the *Empire Builder* would provide travellers with a sense of hope. The notion that the Great Northern was there with a transcontinental service provided pre-Depression comfort, and it was a service that could be relied upon. The Great Northern tightened up the schedule on its signature train. During the 1930s, the westbound *Empire Builder* made the run from Chicago to Seattle in 58 hours, 45 minutes, and returned in 56 hours, 25 minutes.

The fact that the *Empire Builder* survived the Great Depression is a testament to the success of the concept and to the commitment by the Great Northern to keep it running. The *Oriental Limited*, on the other hand, was not so lucky. It was quietly terminated in March 1931.

FOUR

The Great Northern and Glacier National Park

To this day, the identities of the *Empire Builder* and Glacier National Park are inextricably linked. The Great Northern literally put the park on the map and helped define its image and relationship with its visitors in a way that is still seen to this day. No mention of the history of the railroad or the park is complete without mention of the other.

In the days before the United States had a network of transcontinental paved highways, American railroads allowed visitors to reach the great national parks of the West. The Atchison, Topeka & Santa Fe is linked to the early development of Grand Canyon National Park. The Union Pacific played the same role for Colorado's Rocky Mountain National Park, just as the Northern Pacific did for Yellowstone National Park. The mighty Southern Pacific was linked to the promotion of Yosemite National Park, even though it was the short-line Yosemite Valley Railroad that actually ran into the park.

In each of the above instances, travelers actually reached the respective parks by bus or a spur line. None of the great transcontinental railroads directly touched a national park with their main line, except for the Great Northern. It ran along the park's perimeter for 60 miles. The schedule of the *Empire Builder* was specifically timed so that the train made its run in daylight.

Glacier National Park encompasses 1,013,572 acres of mountains, lakes, alpine meadows, and glaciers straddling the Continental Divide; the great naturalist George Bird Grinnell called it "the Crown of the Continent." It was thanks to

The heart of the Rockies in Glacier National Park was George Bird Grinnell's "Crown of the Continent." Also captivated by this mountain majesty, James Jerome Hill became a major proponent of its national park status. His trains brought people to see Glacier, and his son Louis built the infrastructure to pamper park visitors once they arrived. The mountains are Mount Oberlin on the left, Mount Cannon on the right, and Clements Mountain in the center. The Continental Divide runs left to right on this side of Clements. *Bill Yenne*

Opened in 1913, the Glacier Park Lodge was the first of Louis Hill's grand hotels for Glacier National Park. It was located on Great Northern right-of-way, just outside the park. The Glacier Park Station is to the right and out of view. Passengers alighting here walked through the gate structure at the right and then up the walkway to the main entrance of the hotel. *Author collection*

Grinnell's efforts—and those of Jim Hill, who inundated Congress with a public relations blitz—that Glacier became America's 10th national park on May 11, 1910.

Hill and Grinnell, the industrialist and the environmentalist, made strange bedfellows, but they both saw the value in preserving the Crown of the Continent from exploitation by mining and lumbering interests. Both saw the value in setting aside a place purely for the intrinsic beauty, but for Hill, the value was monetary. Tourists liked to look at intrinsic beauty, and they needed to buy a ticket on the Great Northern in order to get there.

In the 1890s, not long after the completion of the Great Northern's transcontinental line, the railroad's passengers disembarked at Belton on the west side of the Continental Divide to visit the scenery in what became Glacier National Park. Many took the short stagecoach ride to Lake McDonald, the largest lake in what is now the park. Tourist facilities had begun to take shape at the foot of the lake, thanks to early settlers such as Charlie Howe and Milo Apgar. Near the head of the lake, George Snyder built a small hotel in 1895. Nevertheless, tourist facilities were rather spartan in the Lake McDonald area and nonexistent elsewhere. The Empire Builder decided that the Great Northern should do something about this.

Official National Park Service photographer George Alexander Grant took this picture of the *Empire Builder* pulling into Glacier Park Station on June 12, 1934. The 4-8-2 motive power on the train is a Great Northern Class P-2 that was built by the Baldwin Locomotive Works in October 1923 and used on the *Empire Builder* for more than a decade. *National Park Service*

The dominant theme adopted by Louis Hill for his Glacier National Park hostelries was the Swiss chalet. The architecture was Swiss-inspired, and so were the uniforms worn by the service staff in the 1930s. These young ladies were photographed by George Alexander Grant at the Going-to-the-Sun Chalets on Upper St. Mary Lake on July 5, 1933. The cloud-topped mountain directly behind them is Dusty Star. *National Park Service*

The guiding force in the Great Northern immersing itself in the infrastructure of Glacier National Park was not Jim Hill, but his son Louis. In fact, this project excited Louis more than the day-to-day business of running his father's railroad. He had visited Glacier before it was Glacier National Park and he returned often. In the summer of 1910, just after the park was designated,

The Great Northern Logo

Like most trademarks, Great Northern's symbol and slogan were products of evolution. The first slogan, which was developed in 1890, was "Great Northern Railway Line." In 1894 "Line" was dropped, and a year later "Great Northern Railway" appeared in a rectangular monogram.

In 1911, as the Great Northern opened its hotels and chalets in Glacier National Park in Montana, Louis Warren Hill coined the advertising slogan "See America First," which appeared in quotation marks above the logo. Below the railway name was "National Park Route." In 1914, "Glacier National Park" was substituted for "National Park Route" in the rectangular trademark.

The Rocky Mountain goat, which is really an antelope, first appeared in Great Northern's trademark in 1921. Former company president William P. Kenney is credited with suggesting the inclusion of the bewhiskered animal in the symbol. Kenney's suggestion was prompted by the many Rocky Mountain goats in Glacier National Park. Adopted as the "mascot" of the Great Northern, the goat in the logo was nicknamed "Rocky."

From 1921 to 1936, the appearance of the trademark was slightly altered, but there were many variations of the wording around the edge of the circle. In 1936, the profile silhouette of the goat replaced the full-faced "Rocky," and the words "Great Northern Railway" were added to the circle. An outer band of black subsequently was strengthened, but beyond this, the trademark remained unchanged for the next 31 years.

In 1967, the Great Northern adopted the corporate identification program that resulted in the adoption of the new "Big Sky Blue" corporate color. The new, modernized Rocky was described as "younger and more vigorous." The word "Railway" was dropped, and the phrase "Great Northern" appeared separate from, but kept in a precisely defined relationship to, the circular symbol.

This sample sticker is characteristic of the many items bearing a cartoon likeness of Rocky that the Great Northern produced for internal use. This one was designed to be used in nonpublic areas of the *Empire Builder* to exhort the staff to be courteous to the passengers. *Author collection*

This is the interior of the main lobby at the Glacier Park Lodge as it appeared in 1915, shortly after the facility opened. The Japanese lantern motif was adopted in an effort to tie the hotel thematically to the *Oriental Limited*, the Great Northern's signature transcontinental luxury train at that time. Today the lobby is still essentially the same, although the decor has changed slightly and gentlemen are no longer expected to wear ties. *Author collection*

he was onsite and planned for a network of hostelries throughout Glacier. Louis' plan for hotels in the park was the most ambitious of any such strategy for an American national park.

In 1911, Louis Hill approved the phrase "See America First" as an advertising slogan to entice well-heeled travelers onto the Great Northern lines rather than onto transoceanic steamships. He wanted tourists from the East to look west into their own land rather than across the Atlantic to Europe.

Soon, Louis' ambitious building program was underway. In its first full year of existence, the federal government's total budget for Glacier National Park was

This 1915 advertisement shows a happy young lady horsing around near the Belton Chalets. The place where her horse is standing would be right in the middle of the Great Northern tracks. The ad brags that eight of railroad's hostelries were already in business. *Author collection*

The Belton Chalets were the first Great Northern Railway hostelry to open near Glacier National Park. Like the Glacier Park Lodge, they were on railroad property just outside the park boundary. The Glacier Park Lodge was at the east entrance to the park, while the Belton Chalets anchored the west side. *Author collection*

The native people of the West "Saw America First," and now it was your turn, thanks to the Great Northern Railway. Louis Hill coined the phrase "See American First" in 1911, and the railroad used it as the catch phrase to package its marketing of its growing number of tourist facilities in Glacier National Park. The hotel in the sketch is the Many Glacier. *Author collection*

$15,000, but the Great Northern invested more than six times that sum in east-side road construction alone. Except for the existing properties at Lake McDonald, the National Park Service granted the exclusive hotel concession to the Great Northern Railway, and Louis Hill did not disappoint them. Until World War II, the railroad spent more money on infrastructure in the park than the National Park Service.

During the first two years that Glacier was a national park, Hill constructed the first buildings in an eventual 34-room chalet complex adjacent to the Great Northern depot at Belton, and another inside the park at Two Medicine Lake, 12 miles north of East Glacier.

On the west side of the Continental Divide, a dozen miles from Belton, John Lewis built a large hotel to replace the Lake McDonald hotel. Because of this, Louis decided to build the modest chalet complex on the west side at Belton and establish his first two major grand hotels on the east side. In any case, the east side was that much closer to Chicago and the Twin Cities. These east side hotels were the Glacier Park Lodge at Midvale (originally known as Glacier Park Hotel) and the Many Glacier Hotel on Lake McDermott (now Swiftcurrent Lake), 59 miles to the north.

The Glacier Park Lodge was located at the point just outside the park where the westbound main line of the Great Northern first intersected the park boundary, while the Many Glacier Hotel was within the park in a spectacular setting that Hill had selected in 1909, and described as being like Switzerland. Naturally, the architecture of the lodges were a Swiss alpine theme. In addition to these grand lodges, Hill planned a network of smaller chalets throughout the park.

Cabin camps were installed at East Glacier, and construction of the Glacier

In 1925, the Great Northern Railway was still "The Route of the *Oriental Limited*," but at Glacier National Park it was just four seasons away from becoming the "Route of the *Empire Builder*." The first paragraph in the copy alludes to Triple Divide Peak in Glacier National Park, the only place in North America with drainage into three oceans. *Author collection*

This Great Northern "See America First" advertisement appeared shortly after Many Glacier Hotel opened in 1915. It pictures a corner of the hotel with Swiftcurrent Lake and Grinnell Point in the background. Snowcapped Swiftcurrent Mountain is in the center, and Mount Wilbur is on the right. The White Motor Company touring cars of the Great Northern–owned Glacier Park Transportation Company were already a selling point. Blackfeet Chief Three Bears invites the reader to "Meet me at Glacier National Park this summer." Initially, the Blackfeet were as amused by the tourists as the tourists were fascinated by the Blackfeet. *Author collection*

Built by the Great Northern and opened in 1915, the Many Glacier Hotel remains the largest hotel located within Glacier National Park. The lobby affords extraordinary views of peaks such as Mount Gould on the left and Grinnell Point on the right. Originally promoted by the Great Northern, saddle horse excursions are still a popular activity for guests at Many Glacier. The hotel is also located at the nexus of many valleys, each with scenic trails. *Author collection*

Park Lodge began in April 1912. Fifty railroad carloads of Douglas fir logs were brought in from Oregon and Washington for the hotel. The largest logs, which formed pillars for the grand, six-story lobby, weighed 50 tons each. They were almost six feet in diameter and 52 feet long. Designed by architect Samuel Bartlett, the hotel cost over $500,000 and took almost two years to construct. The main section opened in June 1913, and an annex was added the following winter. The lobby alone measured 200 by 100 feet, and there was also a dining room and 155 guest rooms, including those in the main building and the annex. In September 1913, the great Empire Builder himself, James Jerome Hill, celebrated his 75th birthday at the Glacier Park Lodge.

Initially, the decor of the lobby and dining room at the Glacier Park Lodge featured Japanese lanterns and an oriental motif to dovetail with the marketing theme of the Great Northern's *Oriental Limited*, but by the time the *Empire Builder* became the Great Northern's signature streamliner, the theme of the hotel had evolved to reflect what visitors most expected, American Indians. The hotel was located adjacent to where the park boundary adjoined the Blackfeet Reservation.

In the summer of 1913, Hill had eight small Swiss-style chalets in service at Many Glacier, and the following year, work began on the great lodge, which was

Published by A. J. Dickinson, the Great Northern's passenger traffic manager, *Vacations For All* was one of the most popular vacation brochures ever issued for an American national park. *Author collection*

destined to be Glacier's largest. The architect was Thomas McMahon, and Louis Hill was intimately involved in the design process. Unlike the Glacier Park Lodge, which used timber from the Pacific Northwest, the Many Glacier Hotel was built almost entirely with cedar and other materials from the local area. Almost all of the hotel's woodwork, including the furniture, utilized native timber. The stone foundation for Many Glacier was built with local rock. More than two million board feet of lumber was cut from the forest east of the hotel, and a sawmill built on the site turned out finished lumber. In fact, the only fully prefinished woodwork brought to the hotel site were window sashes and door frames.

The Many Glacier Hotel opened on July 4, 1915. It may have had a rustic appearance, but it was outfitted with comforts and conveniences such as telephones, hot and cold running water, steam heat, and electric lights. As with the Glacier Park Lodge, the basic facility was augmented by additional buildings, which were completed in 1918.

By 1915, under Louis Hill's direction, the Great Northern built Swiss style chalets at Cut Bank Creek and at Sun Point on St. Mary Lake, which were between East Glacier and Many Glacier.

Empire Builder Dining Car Recipes:

Spaghetti a la Glacier Park

(As prepared by Steve Kogl,
who had 32 years of service on the *Empire Builder*.
When asked "What constitutes a perfect meal?"
He replied, "Good food cooked correctly
and served tastily.")

- 2 ounces bacon
- 1/2 ounce garlic
- 2 ounces ham fat
- 1 ounce green pepper
- 4 ounces onion

(All these ingredients to be chopped fine)

Braise all together with ham bone and one can of tomatoes. Cook for one hour. Strain and mix with cooked spaghetti. Season to taste. Serve in casserole with Parmesan cheese and minced chicken.

This Great Northern advertisement appearing in 1940 celebrated the notion of the honorary Waterton-Glacier International Peace Park and featured a photograph taken from Waterton's Great Northern– owned Prince of Wales Hotel. *Author collection*

By 1941, cartoon mountain goats were starting to figure prominently in the Great Northern's advertising for "Route of the *Empire Builder*" to Glacier National Park. Customers were also being offered a "Pay Later" plan. This was Glacier's last season for five years. The United States was about to enter World War II, and the park's hotels were closed for the duration. *Author collection*

Construction had to surmount Glacier's obstacles. In the case of the Going-to-the-Sun Chalets at Sun Point, logs were cut at the upper end of St. Mary Lake, floated in rafts down the lake, then hauled up a cliff to the construction site. These hostelries, like those previously mentioned, were all accessible by paved roads, but Louis Hill had an even more ambitious project in mind.

Even as work was progressing on his grand hotels and network of chalets, Louis Hill was planning a series of chalets deep in the backcountry of Glacier National Park at locations that were, and still are, accessible only on foot or horseback. The seeds for this scheme were sewn in Louis' imagination by Lyman Sperry, a professor at Oberlin College in Ohio with dual specialties in zoology and biology. In 1896 Louis Hill encouraged Sperry to survey the interior of what became Glacier National Park. Among his expeditions was a crossing of the Continental Divide from Lake McDonald to St. Mary Lake by way of Gunsight Pass.

In the course of his work, Sperry discovered the glacier that was later named for him, surveyed what became Glacier's most spectacular backcountry trail, and

By 1945, the Great Northern's cartoon "Rocky" was sad and lonely. The "Route of the *Empire Builder*" still ran past the park, but the Great Northern's tourist facilities had been dark since before the United States entered the war. Rocky and his railroad wanted the war to be won so that everyone could have some summer fun in Montana. *Author collection*

gave Louis Hill suggestions for two backcountry lodges. A chalet at Gunsight Lake, east of the Continental Divide was completed in 1911, and the Sperry Chalets, near Sperry Glacier, opened in 1914. The end of the largest structure in the complex has the letters "G.N.Ry." (Great Northern Railway) laid out in light-colored stone that contrasts with the dark red stone of the rest of the structure.

Meanwhile, the Great Northern Railway paid for the construction of the Gunsight Pass Trail. In 1915, another high-country facility, Granite Park Chalets,

was completed on the Swiftcurrent Pass Trail leading from Lake McDonald to Many Glacier. Both Sperry and Granite Park Chalets presented a challenge. Since they were above the timberline, stone, instead of log, structures were required. Great Northern Railway quarrying crews worked on site to build the completely native stone structures. Other materials, ranging from cement to furniture to food, came up from below on 60-horse pack strings. The Gunsight Chalets were destroyed in a massive avalanche in 1916 and were never rebuilt, but both the Sperry and Granite Park Chalets are still in service in the twenty-first century and still reachable only by trail.

What is perhaps most amazing about the two major grand lodges and nine smaller chalets that Louis Hill built in Glacier National Park was not that

Opened in 1914 at Lake McDonald, John Lewis' hotel was sold to the Great Northern Railway in 1930. Lewis was an avid hunter and the lobby included items from his immense collection of stuffed wildlife that he had hunted himself or had received through trade. Today, the lobby still contains many of these items and similar ones that were acquired to replace ones that have gone missing through the years. *Author collection*

they were built in some of the most difficult terrain imaginable, but that they were all in service in the space of just five years. It is a testament to the can-do work ethic that was the standard operating procedure for the engineers and builders of the Great Northern.

America's railroads were often maligned for their greed during the early decades of the twentieth century, but the Great Northern must be given full credit for the enormous investment it made in the infrastructure of Glacier National Park, an infrastructure that long outlived the railroad's involvement in Glacier and the life of the railroad itself.

In 1913, Louis Hill had proposed building a third grand hotel in the spirit of Glacier Park and Many Glacier in Waterton Lakes National Park, which is contiguous with Glacier National Park, but located north of the border in the Canadian province of Alberta. Delayed by World War I, this project was finally underway in 1926 and opened in July 1927. It was named Edward, Prince of Wales, for the popular heir apparent to the British throne who owned property near Waterton.

Yellowstone, Yosemite, and the Grand Canyon each have its singular signature great lodge—the Old Faithful Inn, the Ahwahnee, and El Tovar. By the time that the *Empire Builder* made its first run, Glacier and Waterton had four. Within a year of the *Empire Builder's* debut, all of the four were owned and operated by the Great Northern's Glacier Park Hotel Company (later Glacier Park Company). Louis Hill built three and bought the fourth. When the rival Chicago, Milwaukee & St. Paul Railroad approached John Lewis about his 64-room grand hotel at Lake McDonald, Hill and the Great Northern Board of Directors were shaken into action. The deal was closed in time for the 1930 season.

In 1931, members of the Rotary Clubs of Alberta and Montana suggested joining the two parks as a symbol of the peace and friendship between the two countries. In 1932, the United States and Canadian governments voted to designate

The Great Northern's 1946 advertising campaign celebrated the reopening of the Glacier National Park hotels. Hitler was gone, the "Route of the *Empire Builder*" once again led to "Somewhere west of worry," and Rocky had a smile on his white-whiskered face. *Author collection*

Waterton and Glacier as Waterton Glacier International Peace Park. It was an honorary rather than administrative designation. The parks are both now recognized as biosphere reserves and were named as World Heritage Sites in 1995.

In 1932, the completion of the Going-to-the-Sun Road through the center of Glacier National Park and across Logan Pass opened the heart of the park to many more visitors. Sections of the park that previously had taken days of horseback riding to see could now be driven through in a few hours. The Great Northern–owned Glacier Park Company introduced a fleet of bright red Jammer buses, built by the White Motor Company, to take park visitors on one of the most spectacular drives in North America. Tour packages brought tourists into either East Glacier or Belton on Great Northern's new *Empire Builder*, then by road through the park to the opposite station. Accommodations were at Great Northern Glacier Park Company hotels.

In 1911, Louis Hill had planned only to involve the Great Northern Railway in the Glacier National Park hotel business for only a few years, but it was an involvement that spanned half a century. Historian Michael Ober wrote that during this 50-year period, "The Great Northern gave to Glacier the housing it needed, the advertisement and notoriety that it demanded."

The Great Northern adopted "Rocky," the Rocky Mountain goat, as the logo for its railroad and its operations in Glacier National Park. Rocky still survives as the logo for Glacier Park, Incorporated, which operates the hotels and the famous fleet of Red Buses that Louis Hill introduced in the 1930s. In this picture, a real Rocky poses warily before a Red Bus at Logan Pass in the center of the park. Also nicknamed "Jammers" because of the frequent gear changes required in crossing the steep mountains, the Red Buses were built by the White Motor Company and updated by Ford in the 1990s. *Bill Yenne*

FIVE

The New *Empire Builder* and the Mid-Century

In 1944, as the Allied victory in World War II seemed probable, the thoughts of American consumers and companies turned to making optimistic projections of what the American way of life would be in the postwar world. Against this backdrop, the Great Northern Railway proudly announced that five completely new *Empire Builder*s would go into service between Chicago and the Pacific "as soon as they could be assembled."

Despite the Great Depression of the 1930s, the Great Northern survived as the premier American railroad serving the Pacific Northwest. During World War II, the railway flourished as a military supply line. All-time records for annual freight traffic were set in 1942, 1943, and 1944. Record highs for passenger volume were recorded in 1944 and 1945. In 1944, ton miles (a ton mile equals the movement of a ton of freight one mile) totaled 19.6 billion. In 1945, passenger miles (each represents transportation of one passenger one mile) amounted to 1.3 billion.

This heavy wartime traffic was handled by a growing number of diesel and steam locomotives, and by electric motive power on the Cascade Division. Improvement of other railway facilities also continued and were subject to wartime shortages, but with the war's end, this program was accelerated.

In 1926, the Great Northern was the first railroad serving the Northwest to operate a diesel locomotive, although it was acquired for use in the Twin Cities terminal area. It was a 600-horsepower oil-electric switch engine jointly manufactured by General Electric, Ingersoll-Rand, and the American Locomotive Company (Alco). However, early mainline diesel operations were slow in coming. The

A pair of Great Northern E-7 (E7A) diesels head north along Puget Sound with a 10-car *Empire Builder*. The lead unit was delivered by the Electro-Motive Division in April 1945 and numbered 501B by the railroad. It was renumbered as 503 in 1952. *Author collection*

This advertisement from the General Motors Electro-Motive Division featured one of the manufacturer's E7A units and gave a plug to the Great Northern's New *Empire Builder*. The unit, pictured here, was the first Great Northern E7A, delivered as No. 500A in 1945. Designated as an E-7, it was renumbered in 1952. *Author collection*

BETTER TRAINS FOLLOW GENERAL MOTORS LOCOMOTIVES

GM GENERAL MOTORS LOCOMOTIVES

The new EMPIRE BUILDER, completely streamlined train running daily each way between Chicago and Seattle-Portland, is the Great Northern's "Greatest Train." This service is headed by General Motors Diesel locomotives.

IT'S a matter of record that most of America's finest and fastest trains are powered by General Motors Diesel locomotives.

You'll find a General Motors Diesel up front, for example, on the sumptuous Empire Builder and more than 150 other de luxe high-speed limiteds and streamliners whose names are famous from coast to coast.

The fact is, four out of five of all Diesel locomotives in passenger service, and nine out of ten hauling the new fast freights, bear the General Motors name plate.

Why do General Motors Diesels enjoy such a commanding preference among the nation's railroads?

One reason is that General Motors pioneered the Diesel mainline locomotive in 1934, making possible the modern Diesel-powered train that has revolutionized railway travel. Since then General Motors has built locomotive units totaling more than 5,000,000 Diesel horsepower, an experience unmatched in railroading.

This tremendous backlog of experience explains General Motors' leadership in design that enables trains to maintain faster "on time" schedules in all weather behind General Motors Diesels, and give the public a cleaner, smoother, more restful ride.

It explains, too, why most of the new luxury trains the railroads are now building have General Motors Diesel locomotives on order. For both the railroads and the public agree that *"better trains follow General Motors locomotives"!*

ELECTRO-MOTIVE DIVISION

GENERAL MOTORS • LA GRANGE, ILL.

Home of the Diesel Locomotive

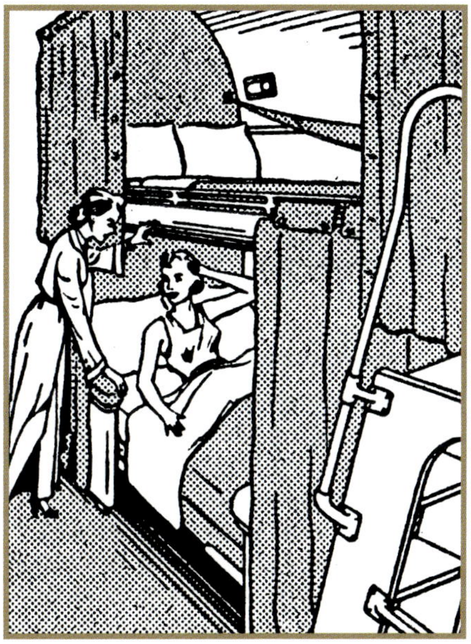

By day, the Pullman berths in the *Empire Builder* were full-width, form-fitting seats with latex rubber cushions and arm rests. Wide picture windows were very popular. By night, the upper and lower berths offered low-sag springs and latex foam rubber mattresses. Reading lights and clothes hangers were also included. *Author collection*

Chicago, Burlington & Quincy began operating its *Pioneer Zephyr* diesel passenger service in 1934, but by the time of World War II, most American passenger trains were still pulled by steam locomotives. For the Great Northern, the powerhouses were the Class N 2-8-8-0 steam units, originally acquired from the Baldwin Locomotive Works in 1912, but upgraded to N-3 standard between 1940 and 1942. Nevertheless, the nature of motive power for passenger service was about to change.

The earliest diesels on the Great Northern were mainly switch engines, but technology was rapidly changing. In 1940, the Electro-Motive Division of General Motors unveiled the prototype for its new bulldog-nosed Class FT diesel locomotives. The FT demonstrator, No. 103, was a 45-ton, four-unit freight diesel with a maximum tractive effort of 228,000 pounds, compared to 118,400 for the N-3 steam equipment. During a demonstration run in March 1940, the Great Northern used the FT unit to carry a 5,000-ton freight from Wenatchee, Washington, to Minneapolis at an average speed of 31 miles per hour. This was roughly the speed of the much lighter *Empire Builder* using the S-2 Class 4-8-4 steam locomotive. The Great Northern also tried No. 103 on the demanding iron ore run and lugged a 16,000-ton freight between Kelly Lake and the Great Lakes docks at Superior, Wisconsin. The locomotive was then switched to passenger service between Duluth and the Twin Cities.

The Great Northern liked what it saw in the streamlined Class FT diesels, not only in terms of power, but in terms of efficiency. The new diesel was more economical to operate and had about half the down time of a heavy steam locomotive. Five operational FTA units were built for the Great Northern in 1941, but the United States' entry into World War II delayed subsequent deliveries because General Motors was swamped with war production. Two FTAs were built in 1943, and 24 were added to the roster in 1944. Eventually, the Great Northern was the largest operator in the United States, with 52 FTA cab units and 45 FTB

The Electro-Motive Division E7A (E-7) locomotives delivered 2,000 horsepower and were typically used in pairs rather than combined with an unmanned power unit. The Class F diesels, on the other hand, typically operated on the Great Northern with two cab units and a power unit. *Author collection*

power units. For the duration of World War II, the FTs were used primarily in freight service in the Cascade Division out of Wenatchee and on the Kalispell Division to boost heavy freights across Marias Pass.

While most of the passenger diesels that the Great Northern acquired for the *Empire Builder* and its sister streamliners were Electro-Motive Division Class F equipment, the first 13 Great Northern passenger diesels were the Electro-Motive Division Class E units, specifically E7s, including E7A cab units and uncrewed E7B power units. The E7s each delivered 2,000 horsepower compared to 1,350 horsepower for the FT, and 1,500 horsepower for the later Class F locomotives. The E units differed from the F units in that they had an A1A-A1A six-axle configuration, as opposed to the B-B–type four-axle configuration of the F Class. The E units had a more deeply slanted nose than the F units, except for the E7 and E8 units, which resembled the F units.

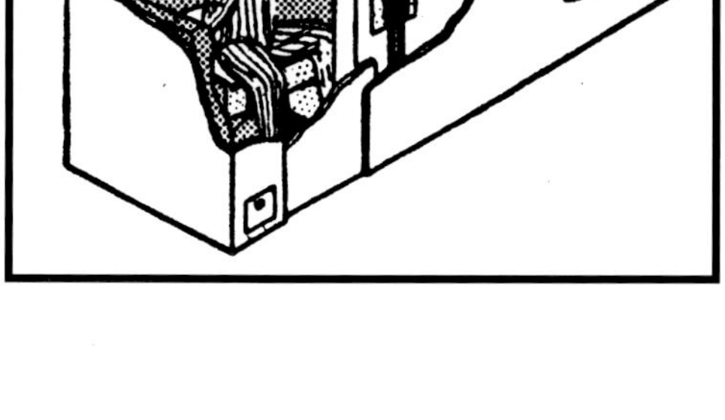

The Duplex Roomettes on the *Empire Builder* were compact, completely private rooms that were designed for single occupancy and were only 10 percent more than the cost of a lower berth. At night, premade full-size beds folded out. There was a private wash basin and toilet, as well as individual room temperature control. *Author collection*

Empire Builder Dining Car Recipes:

Baked Columbia River Salmon

(As prepared by Chef Homer Russell. Russell had 38 years of service on the *Empire Builder*. "To know is but a part," Russell said. "Skillful expression of knowledge is perfection.")

Cut fish in desired pieces and place in well-buttered pan.Add salt and pepper, and a little flour to thicken; sprinkle with butter. Add a little stock, about 1/2 pint for two portions, prepared from bones and trimmings. Place in moderate oven and bake until done.

Fish dinners served on Great Northern dining cars were delightful because of the great varieties of fish produced along the lines. From the lakes of Minnesota, the Great Northern served whitefish, lake trout, northern pike, bass, and perch. Mountain trout came from private hatcheries in Montana, while salmon, halibut, black cod, and deep sea crabs came from the Pacific Ocean. Olympia oysters were harvested at the lower end of Puget Sound.

For this reason, all of the E and F units operated by the Great Northern looked similar.

The first four passenger E7s for the Great Northern were built by the Electro-Motive Division in April 1945, and were followed by six additional E7s in June of that year. The final three of the class were built in August 1947. In its internal classification system, the Great Northern inserted a hyphen and called them E-7 units. In service on the *Empire Builder*, they were used in pairs and delivered a total of 4,000 horsepower for a 12-car *Empire Builder* train.

With the arrival of the E-7s, the Great Northern adopted its distinctive new passenger color scheme of brilliant Omaha Orange, trimmed in Pullman Green, and separated by a narrow stripe of metallic gold paint. This livery was known as the *Empire Builder* color scheme, although it was used for both passenger and freight motive power and on passenger trains other than the *Empire Builder*.

The legendary Omaha Orange livery of the postwar *Empire Builder* was actually the first standardized color that was adopted by the Great Northern, other than the solid Pullman Green of the earlier passenger cars. Prior to World War II, steam locomotives appeared in a variety of colors, including black and green, and often in combinations of the two. Boilers often appeared in light green or light grey. Omaha Orange was the result of a search for a high visibility color and was chosen after tests carried out in the early 1940s. The paint was manufactured by DuPont for the Electro-Motive Division, who designated the color as GM31. The name Omaha Orange was apparently chosen for its alliterative charm. H. J. Searles, the Great Northern's general safety supervisor, wrote in *RailwayAge* magazine in June 1932, "We [the Great Northern] have found this color combination excellent, not only for track visibility, but for maintenance and general good looks."

Daily departures by the *Empire Builder* used the new Omaha Orange E-7 units beginning on February 23, 1947, and offered a 45-hour schedule between Chicago on the east, and Seattle and Portland on the west. With this, the Great Northern became the first northern transcontinental system to inaugurate diesel streamliner service.

These were also the first transcontinental trains to operate completely new sleeping cars and coaches built in the United States after the end of World War II. Within these cars were new style Day-Nite coaches and new duplex roomettes. The bedrooms and drawing rooms were improved. Like the locomotives, the *Empire Builder*'s passenger cars were painted in Omaha Orange and trimmed in Pullman Green and metallic gold. With all of this, the Great Northern's advertising began referring to the service as the "New" *Empire Builder*.

The arrival of the New *Empire Builder* coincided with the advent of the first measurable vacation traffic on the railroads of the United States since the summer before Pearl Harbor. The Great Northern was there to take advantage of this sudden explosion of pent-up demand. The year 1946 marked the first season since 1941 that the Glacier National Park hostelries were back in service. The Great Northern dusted off its luxury hotels and rustic chalets and rolled out the red carpets at the steps of the New *Empire Builder* at the Belton and East Glacier stations.

With the acquisition of all the new equipment for the New *Empire Builder*, the Great Northern had many used passenger cars that could be recycled. In order to make use of these cars, the company revived the long retired *Oriental Limited* name. Having been honorably discharged as a name train in the 1931, the *Oriental Limited* brand was reinstated in 1947, and assigned to the six non-streamliner trains created from the equipment that had previously been used on the *Empire Builder*. The revived *Oriental Limited* service remained in operation for four years.

This 1948 Great Northern advertisement used cartoon Rockys to promote the comfort of the streamlined *Empire Builder*. This illustration also shows the paint scheme used on the top of the E7A (E-7) diesels. The Pullman Green extended only partway. The top of the cab was painted Omaha Orange. *Author collection*

Shortly after the acquisition of its first E-7 units, the Great Northern started to receive its first Electro-Motive Division Class F equipment, specifically F3 locomotives. The bulldog-nosed F3A diesel cab units were augmented by the F3B uncrewed passenger booster power units. As typically configured for passenger service, two of each delivered a aggregate of 6,000 horsepower. The Great Northern bought F3As for freight applications, the *Empire Builder,* and other passenger

trains. In addition, 11 F3Bs were used for freight trains and 13 were acquired for passenger service.

A subtle, but noticeable, difference between E and F units during this time was the livery. Both were painted in Omaha Orange with Pullman Green trim, but the cab tops of the E units, beginning several feet behind the cab, were orange with green tops that matched the tops of all the passenger cars in the train. The F units, on the other hand, had green tops all the way back from the green windshield frames.

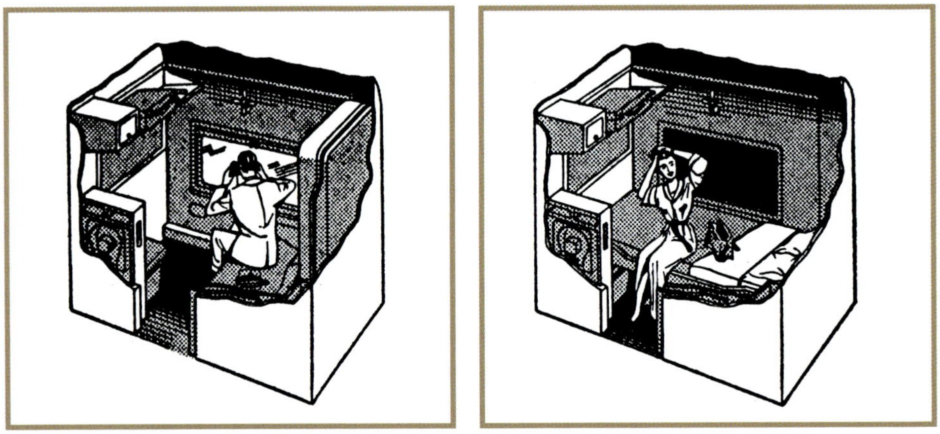

The Roomettes on the *Empire Builder* were promoted as having "all the advantages of the Duplex Roomette plus extra roominess." They had a private wash basin and toilet, individually controlled temperature, plus a full-length mirror and extra baggage space. At night, the "Fold-in-the-Wall" bed folded out of the wall. *Author collection*

This family photo depicts the first five Electro-Motive Division E7A units delivered to the Great Northern. Designed for wide use as a publicity shot, the image was heavily retouched and given crisp logos so it reproduced well in newspapers. *Author collection*

The Electro-Motive Division built the first three F3As for the Great Northern's passenger service in November 1946, and these were followed by six more in October 1947. The last passenger F3A for the Great Northern was built in October 1948.

The F3 units were, in turn, augmented by the F7 units, which were nearly identical except for small differences, mainly in their internal electrical systems. Externally, the two types are distinguished mainly by the F7's large, continuous top filter grille, although some F3s also had the same grille.

In Great Northern nomenclature, the F3s and F7s were grouped together in Class F-3-7-AB for freight and Class P-3-7-AB for passenger service. To avoid confusion, this book uses the F3 and F7 designations when referring to these units. The *A* suffix identifies a cab unit, and the *B* suffix denotes an uncrewed power unit.

The Great Northern acquired the F7s mainly for freight applications. A total of 51 F7As were delivered for freight use, compared to 11 for the *Empire Builder* and her sister trains. In addition, two F3As were rebuilt as F7As. Like the F3A, the F7A diesel cab unit was augmented by a B passenger booster unit. There were 34 F7Bs built for the Great Northern's freight business and 12 F7Bs built for passenger service. The first three Great Northern F7As for passenger use were built in June 1950, and the last two came off the line in June 1952. By this time, the Great

Northern had relegated the E-Units to freight service because the different gear ratios between the E and F locomotives made them difficult to operate together in the same train.

Of all the Class F diesels, the Electro-Motive Division delivered more F7s than all others combined for a total of 2,261 F7As and 1,420 F7Bs sold in the United States alone. An additional 80 F7As and 47 F7Bs were sold in Canada, while 25 F7As and 16 F7Bs were sold in Mexico. The totals for the bulldog-nosed E units were 428 E7As, 82 E7Bs, 418 E8As, and 39 E8Bs. All of these were sold in the United States, except three E8As that the Electro-Motive Division sold in Canada.

Meanwhile, the Great Northern continued to operate electric motive power through the Cascade Tunnel and on the 75

In this advertisement for both the *Empire Builder* and the *Oriental Limited*, the focus was on dining cars and lounge cars. The Great Northern used an E7A (E-7) to represent the *Empire Builder*, and an F3A for the *Oriental Limited*. In fact, it would probably have been the other way around. The *Oriental Limited* name would soon be phased out, as the service would become the *Western Star* in 1951. *Author collection*

The Electro-Motive Division of General Motors delivered the first five operational FTA diesels to the Great Northern in 1941, but further deliveries were interrupted by the United States' entry into World War II. General Motors suddenly needed to fulfill military contracts. This 1943 advertisement promises that a new postwar world is coming and it will be pulled by FTA diesels. Great Northern's first FTAs were originally numbered in the 5000 series that was also used for the road's electrics. *Author collection*

miles of track between Wenatchee and Skykomish, Washington, using a fleet of 18 Y-1 and Z-1 locomotives that had mostly been acquired in the late 1920s before the completion of the tunnel project.

The first Great Northern electric locomotive with a modern look was a Y-1 that was modified in 1945. It had gone off the tracks at the Foss River Bridge on the Cascade Division during World War II while pulling a fast freight loaded with high-priority war materiel. It was rebuilt by the Great Northern in March 1945, retrofitted with an FTA double-cab and body, and painted in the Omaha Orange *Empire Builder* color scheme.

The first new electrics for the Great Northern in nearly two decades, and the last two the company acquired, were built by General Electric in June 1947 with cabs that resembled the Electro-Motive Division Class E diesels. These units were designated as Class W-1 by the Great Northern. They were massive, 5,000-horsepower, 12-axle B-D+D-B double-ended units that were more than 101 feet long. On the W-1 units, the 16 driving wheels and the four-wheel lead trucks on either

Generally similar in appearance and paint scheme to the E7A (E-7) units used on the *Empire Builder*, the bulldog-nosed FTA units were the first operational Great Northern diesels. Deliveries of FTAs that were interrupted in 1941 resumed service in December 1943, with numbering in the 400 series. The Great Northern FTAs served primarily as freight locomotives. *Author collection*

end were equipped with traction motors. This gave these behemoths tremendous pulling power. These were the only two electrics that were delivered from the factory in the *Empire Builder* paint scheme.

The Great Northern made an enormous investment in both motive power and passenger cars during the late 1940s and the early 1950s. In 1949, having just unveiled the New *Empire Builder* in 1947, company president Frank Gavin authorized an $8.4 million upgrade to the fleet. This upgrade included the acquisition of 66 new passenger cars from Pullman and American Car & Foundry to complement the new Electro-Motive Division F7 units on the *Empire Builder*. Mountain Class observation cars with larger windows were included among the cars.

After he ordered the equipment, Gavin turned to his public relations chief Charles Moore, who repackaged the Great Northern's passenger service as the Mid-Century *Empire Builder*.

This 1947 advertisement for the New *Empire Builder* celebrated the style and comfort of new passenger cars. The artist needed to take no license in making the E7A (E-7) diesel look fast and streamlined. For the next two decades, the Great Northern used paintings of the train in the Rockies to promote its *Empire Builder*. *Author collection*

The *Empire Builder* rolls into Wenatchee, Washington, pulled by an F3A unit built for the Great Northern by the Electro-Motive Division in November 1947. This locomotive operated with the *Empire Builder* for two decades. *Gil Hulin*

This advertisement took us inside the New *Empire Builder*, circa 1947, where the 36-seat dining cars were made to appear spacious. How many times did the copywriter use the word "new?" Smoking was permitted, but it apparently was not bothersome. *Author collection*

Inside the cab, Great Northern engineer Clyde Yenne and his fireman guide the *Empire Builder* westward toward East Glacier Station and Glacier National Park beyond. *Author collection*

With a new integrated fleet, a five-train schedule of third generation *Empire Builder* streamliners entered service on June 3, 1951.

Only four years had elapsed since the unveiling of the second-generation New *Empire Builder*. In fact, as nice as this Mid-Century *Empire Builder* was, it wasn't as big as the leap from steam to Class E diesels a few years earlier, but it was designed to feel like it. This was the era when Detroit radically changed its automobile styling every year, and Frank Gavin felt that he had to keep up with the pace. Two sweeping upgrades in a short timespan was unheard of in the industry and was clearly indicative of the expansive postwar U.S. economy. The United States was entering an era of plenty that was unprecedented in its history, and it was travelling across the northern tier of the nation and visiting Glacier National Park in style. The *Empire Builder* was still a 45-hour schedule, but the public was eager to travel, and the *Empire Builder* was always exceptional.

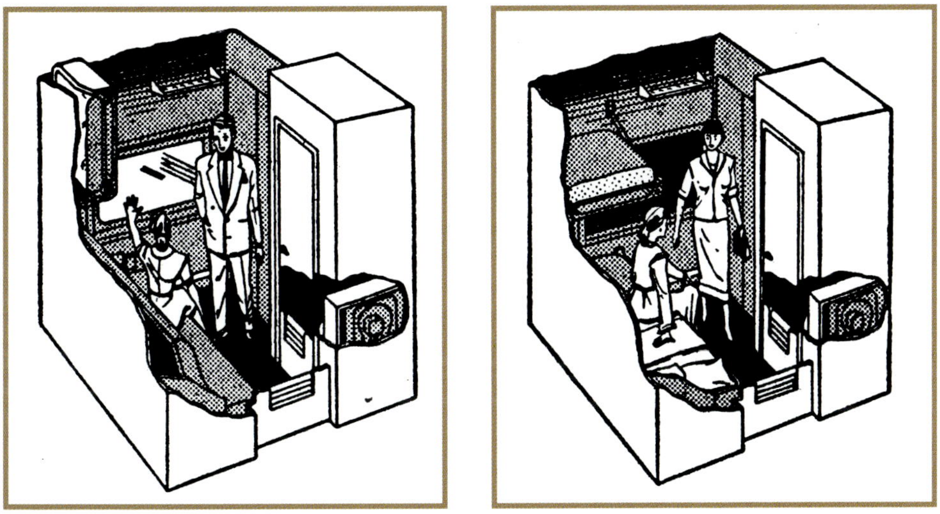

The *Empire Builder* double bedroom was an enclosed private room for one or two persons that was marketed as "ideal for family groups." A super-sofa provided seating for three, and at night there were upper and lower beds. Dressing facilities were included, and most rooms had enclosed toilets. *Author collection*

Each train in this new edition of the classic *Empire Builder* had up to 15 cars and was powered by a pair of F7As with an F7B between to deliver 4,500 aggregate horsepower.

One of the high points of the interior furnishings of the new Mid-Century packaging was the combination coffee shop and lounge car. It was restyled in the Western motif that was in vogue in the mid-twentieth century and was named the G-Bar-N Ranch car. The G-Bar-N offered table seating for 12, plus room for 18 in the lounge and 14 at the bar counter. The G-Bar-N was so popular that when the Great Northern took it off line during the winter of 1955 and 1956, a barrage of passenger complains prompted its quick return to service. It remained on the line until 1967.

On June 3, 1951, as the five Mid-Century *Empire Builder* streamliners entered service, they were complemented by a completely new companion train called the *Western Star*. The *Empire Builder* offered the last word in luxury on the 45-hour run from Chicago to Seattle, and the *Western Star* offered similar amenities on a 58-hour run between those cities by way of Grand Forks, North Dakota, and a side-trip to Great Falls, Montana. Many of the passenger cars that had been acquired for the 1947 second generation *Empire Builder* were then handed down to the *Western Star*, just as the pre-1947 *Empire Builder* equipment had been handed down to the temporarily revived *Oriental Limited*. For all practical purposes, the *Western Star* took over the run and schedule of the *Oriental Limited* in 1951, and that classic name was retired forever. The *Western Star* was so important to the Great Northern that the company used it to make the routine stops at the Glacier National Park gateways instead of the *Empire Builder*.

Between Chicago and St. Paul, the routes of the *Empire Builder* and the *Western Star* were on the route lines of the Chicago, Burlington & Quincy. Between Spokane and Portland, the cars from both trains were part of connecting routes of the Spokane, Portland & Seattle Railway. On the Burlington, the *Empire Builder* was combined with that road's *Afternoon Zephyr* service. The section of the

continued on page 95

Mid-Century Great Northern Passenger Diesel Cab Unit Roster

Class	Loco No.	Later GN No(s).	Later BN No(s).
Built by General Motors Electro-Motive Division (April 1945)			
E7	500A	500	9901
E7	500B	500C/502	9903
E7	501A	501	9902
E7	501B	501C/503	9904
Built by General Motors Electro-Motive Division (June 1945)			
E7	502A	504	N/A
E7	502B	502C/505	9905
E7	503A	506	9906
E7	503B	503C/507	N/A
E7	504A	508	N/A
E7	504B	504C/509	9907
Built by General Motors Electro-Motive Division (November 1946)			
F3A	225	359A	N/A
F3A	226	359C	9710
F3A	227	275A/366C	N/A
Built by General Motors Electro-Motive Division (October 1947)			
F3A	228	360A	N/A
F3A	229	360C	N/A
F3A	230	361A	9714
F3A	231	361C	9716
F3A	260A	366A	9732
F3A	261A	367A	N/A

Class	Loco No.	Later GN No(s).	Later BN No(s).
Built by General Motors Electro-Motive Division (November 1947)			
F3A	350A	None	N/A
F3A	350C	None	N/A
F3A	351A	None	N/A
F3A	351C	None	N/A
F3A	352A	None	N/A
F3A	353A	None	N/A
F3A	353C	None	N/A
Built by General Motors Electro-Motive Division (December 1947)			
F3A	354A	None	N/A
F3A	354C	None	N/A
F3A	355A	None	9700
F3A	355C	None	N/A
F3A	356ANone	N/A	
F3A	356C	None	N/A
F3A	357A	None	N/A
F3A	357C	None	N/A
F3A	358A	None	N/A
F3A	358C	None	9708
Built by General Motors Electro-Motive Division (August 1948)			
E7	510	None	9908
E7	511	None	9909
E7	512	None	9910
Built by General Motors Electro-Motive Division (October 1948)			
F3A	266A	368A	N/A
F3A	267A	369A	N/A
F3A	375C	362A	N/A
F3A	376C	362C	N/A
Built by General Motors Electro-Motive Division (June 1950)			
F7A	268A	370A	9742
F7A	269A	367A	9736
F7A	270A	368C	N/A

Class	Loco No.	Later GN No(s).	Later BN No(s).
Built by General Motors Electro-Motive Division (October 1950)			
F7A	275A	363A	N/A
F7A	275B	363C	9724
F7A	364A	None	9726/704
F7A	364C	None	9728
F7A	365A	None	N/A
F7A	365C	None	N/A
Built by General Motors Electro-Motive Division (June 1952)			
F7A	280A	369C	9740
F7A	281A	370C	9744
Rebuilt from F3A units in 1952			
F7A*	350A	None	N/A
F7A*	360A	None	9712
Built by General Motors Electro-Motive Division (May 1966)			
SDP40	320	None	9850/6394
SDP40	321	None	9851/6395
SDP40	322	None	9852/6396
SDP40	323	None	9853/6397
SDP40	324	None	9854/6398
SDP40	325	None	9855/6399
Built by General Motors Electro-Motive Division (June 1967)			
SDP45	326	None	9856/6592
SDP45	327	None	9857/6593
SDP45	328	None	9858/6594
SDP45	329	None	9859/6595
Built by General Motors Electro-Motive Division (August 1967)			
SDP45	330	None	9860/6596
SDP45	331	None	9861/6597
SDP45	332	None	9862/6598
SDP45	333	None	9863/6599

*F3A units retrofitted as F7A units

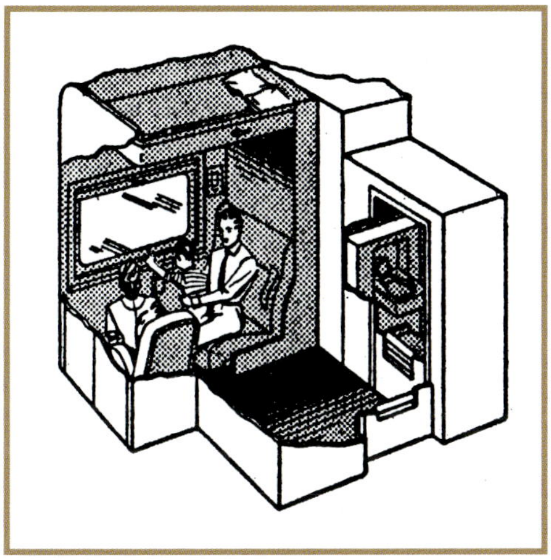

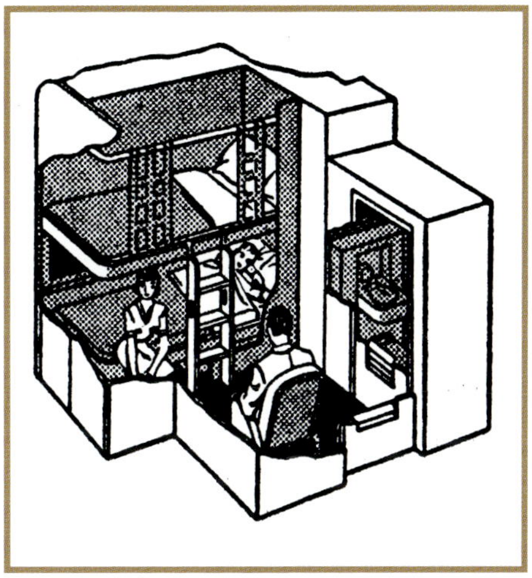

The *Empire Builder's* compartments had a "spacious living room space providing every appointment desired by the fastidious traveller." By day, they offered contoured window seats and movable lounge chairs for dining or card games. An enclosed bathroom and full-size upper and lower beds were also included. *Author collection*

Continued from page 91

Spokane, Portland & Seattle Railway route in the Columbia River Gorge between Pasco and Portland saw cars of the *Empire Builder* combined with those of the rival Northern Pacific's own signature transcontinental, the *North Coast Limited.*

The dining cars on both the *Empire Builder* and the *Western Star* developed a good reputation. They were famous for many specials, but as the Great Northern bragged, "none are more deserving of commendation than their famous baked smoked ham and the delightful sauce served with it." French fried sweet potatoes, bread and butter, coffee, tea, and milk were served with the ham, and the meal cost just 75 cents. The Great Northern proudly proclaimed that it was "a satisfying meal at a reasonable price."

Beginning in 1955, the Great Northern began equipping the *Empire Builder* with the famous dome cars built for the road by the Budd Company. This acquisition, first announced in 1953, was yet another step in the on-going process of continually upgrading the Great Northern's signature streamliner. The short domes went on the line at the end of May and were configured with 46 reclining coach

The *Empire Builder* drawing rooms provided complete privacy for three or four persons travelling together. By day, there was a large sofa, window seat, and movable chair. By night, a folding partition formed two rooms for sleeping privacy. Of course, an enclosed bathroom was included. The engineering that went into creating these accommodations was one of the factors that made the 1950s the golden age of rail travel. *Author collection*

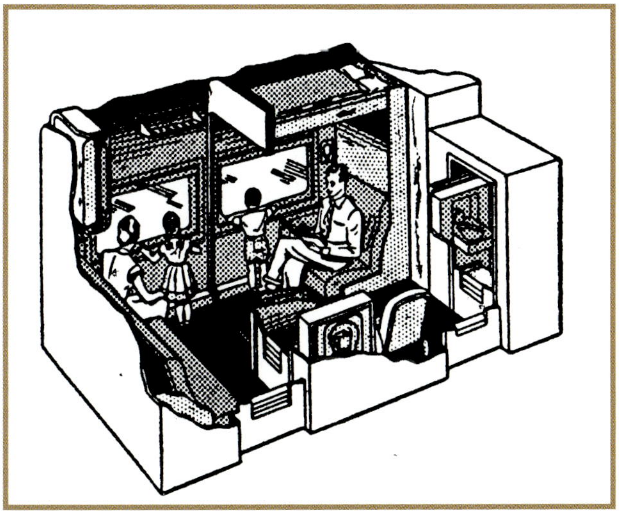

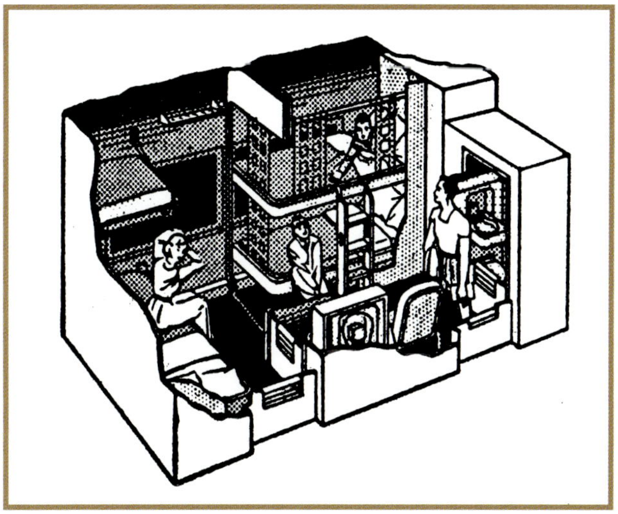

The shiny chrome-trimmed coffee shop on the New *Empire Builder* is captured in 1947, when it was new. A few years later, with the rollout of the Mid-Century edition of the *Empire Builder*, the coffee shop was repackaged and branded as the "G-Bar-N Ranch Car." *BNSF Archives*

seats on their main level and 24 seats upstairs. The big 90-ton Budd Great Dome lounge cars with domes running their full length were added to the fleet in October 1955. All across the Great Northern main line, school children—including myself—ran to the schoolyard fences at recess to wave at the travellers in the dome cars. During the summer, the *Empire Builder* ran with one of the full-length Great Dome lounge cars and three short-domed coach cars. This provided nearly 150 seats in the dome cars, more than was offered on any other streamliner operating on a competing railroad anywhere in the West. In the winter, the trains ran with just two short-domed coaches.

The Budd Company had no relation to either Ralph or John Budd, who were presidents of the Great Northern. It was founded by Edward Gowen Budd in 1912 to build steel frames for automobiles. In the 1930s, he turned to building railcars using a lightweight stainless steel alloy, and he later patented the revolutionary shot-welding process for stainless steel fabrication. One of his first customers was Ralph Budd, who had left the Great Northern in 1931 to head the

Chicago, Burlington & Quincy. For Ralph, Edward developed the stainless-steel *Zephyr* family of streamliners. After the war, the Budd Company pioneered the dome cars that became famous on the *Empire Builder* and other trains.

Within the *Empire Builder's* Great Dome lounge car, there was couch-type seating for 57, plus a 21-seat lounge. It was the height of luxury. There was no better place to sit for the 60-mile run around the southern periphery of Glacier National Park between East Glacier and Belton. The view was so much a part of the theme that the six Budd lounge cars with full-length domes were given names ending in "view" and beginning with one of the sights for which the *Empire Builder* was renowned. They included the *Glacier View*, *Lake View*, *Mountain View*, *Ocean View*, *Prairie View*, and the *River View*.

Downstairs in each of these Great Dome cars was a lounge with a bar and comfortable seating for an additional 32 passengers. Whereas the G-Bar-N Ranch theme predominated in the interior design of that car, the Great Northern chose a Northwest Coast American Indian motif for the interiors of the dome cars. American Indian art, including carvings suggestive of Northwest Coast totem poles, was adapted for wall murals and other details.

The combination lounge and observation club cars that brought up the end of the Mid-Century *Empire Builder* were given names in the coulee series. These included the *Choteau Coulee*, *Corral Coulee*, *Grand Coulee*, *Rocky Coulee*, *Trail Coulee*, and the *Twelve Mile Coulee*. The Great Northern also used a confusing series of naming conventions for other cars on the *Empire Builder*. At one time, sleeping cars

This is one of the last *Empire Builder* advertisements featuring the *Oriental Limited*. The highlight here was on budget travel and promoting the coach class Sleepy Hollow chairs that became Pullman berths with "crisp linens and soft mattresses." *Author collection*

The use of mirrors made the dining car on the 1947 New *Empire Builder* seem to go on forever. Note the framed portrait of James Jerome Hill, which was positioned to be the visual focal point of the room. The table settings matched what the fastidious passenger would expect in the finest restaurant. *BNSF Archives*

were named for glaciers and passes, and observation cars were named for rivers. Later, observation cars were named for mountains, some sleeping cars were renamed for rivers, and the glacier series was dropped. The coulee-series observation cars were actually former river-series cars that were renovated and renamed. Dining cars were named for lakes. Eventually, the mountain-series cars were all transferred from the *Empire Builder* to the *Western Star*.

As with all of the cars in the *Empire Builder*, the dome cars and the observation cars were all painted in the *Empire Builder* color scheme of the Great Northern locomotives that pulled them, but the Great Northern did not own all of them. The Chicago, Burlington & Quincy, upon whose tracks the *Empire Builder* ran between Chicago and St. Paul, owned three short domes, one Great Dome lounge car, and one Great Dome observation car. The Spokane, Portland & Seattle, on whose tracks the *Empire Builder* ran from Spokane to Portland, also owned one of the *Empire Builder* dome cars. The latter company used its own motive power, rather than an *Empire Builder*–configured locomotive, to pull the train on its route.

With the addition of the heavy new Great Dome lounge cars, the Great Northern's motive power package for the Mid-Century *Empire Builder* now included two Electro-Motive Division F7As with a pair of F7B power units

between them. By the middle of the decade, the Mid-Century *Empire Builder* was running a faster schedule of 42 hours, 40 minutes westbound and 44 hours, 30 minutes eastbound. The latter included the time required for an engine change at Havre, Montana, where the big Great Northern diesel maintenance facility was located. Eastbound locomotives were changed there for maintenance so the trains that ran from Havre to St. Paul were pulled by refreshed diesels.

In 1956, the Great Northern made the first major change to the Cascade Tunnel since it had opened the 7.79-mile bore in 1929. The completion of a forced-air ventilation system at the end of July permitted the Great Northern to abandon the electrification on the Cascade Division for the first time since the completion of the first Cascade Tunnel in 1900. This permitted the operation of diesels through

The passenger seats in the 1947 New *Empire Builder* swivelled so that passengers could take advantage of the view beyond the large picture windows. These were the seats that were marketed as Sleepy Hollow seats—passengers could doze off in them. Strange for a Great Northern publicity photo, nobody here looks very happy to be travelling. *BNSF Archives*

The first of the E7A (E-7) locomotives to operate on the Great Northern pulls the *Empire Builder* into Whitefish, Montana, circa 1948. *BNSF Archives*

the tunnel and all the way from Chicago to Seattle for the first time, shaving as much as an hour of switching time off the run's duration. The Great North-ern electric units were then scrapped or sold. The old Class Z-1 locomotives were all scrapped, but the Class Y-1 units were sold to the Pennsylvania Railroad. One of the beautiful and relatively new Class W-1 units was scrapped in 1959, and the other was sold to the Union Pacific. It survived until 1968, when it was cut up.

Meanwhile, Great Northern began to use more electronics. At the railway's data processing center in St. Paul, a state-of-the-art Sperry Univac computer was introduced for such diverse duties as payroll, accounting, labor distribution, and inventory control. The original installation, finished in 1957, made the Great Northern the second among United States railroads to go online and the first among Western railroads. In 1963 the Great Northern installed an updated Univac II computer that could handle an expanded workload. This installation was augmented in 1967 with new hardware in the Great Northern's extensive data processing center. The Univac 418, the railway's first real-time electronic computer, could instantaneously make information available for all facets of the railroad's operations.

Two of these computers were connected with a network of 38 online reporting stations, which were equipped with IBM 1050 data control facilities, thus enabling the railway to immediately pinpoint immediately any one of some 40,000 freight cars on its line.

Extensive use of two-way radio communication in freight train operations and in switching and yard areas began in 1953, and the Great Northern's very high frequency (VHF) radio network between the Twin Cities and the Pacific Coast was completed in early 1956. Radio was thereafter routinely installed on passenger, freight, and yard engines; cabooses; snow-clearing and other maintenance equipment; and on supervisors' rail cars and automobiles.

The 1950s were a golden age for the Mid-Century *Empire Builder,* the Great Northern's signature streamliner. This was the case for the passenger service on most of America's railroads. It was an era of unprecedented prosperity, and the

At first glance, this *Empire Builder* locomotive appears to be an Electro-Motive Division FTA unit, but then you notice that it has a pantograph and is emerging from the Cascade Tunnel. This unit, number 5011, is a single Y-1 that was rebuilt in 1945 after a wartime wreck, and retrofitted by the Great Northern with a double-ended FTA-style cab and body. It was sold to the Pennsylvania Railroad in 1957. The baggage car seen here predates the streamlined look of the post-1947 New *Empire Builder.* *Author collection*

family vacation had become an integral part of the American way of life.

A Ride on the Mid-Century *Empire Builder*

In order to get a better feel for the Mid-Century *Empire Builder*—the definitive edition of the great train—we'll take a highly detailed look at its typical run, with comparisons to the parallel schedule of its sister train, the *Western Star*. In the Mid-Century era, the streamlined *Empire Builder* operated westbound as Great Northern Train 1, and eastbound as Great Northern Train 2. The streamlined *Western Star* operated westbound as Great Northern Train 3, and eastbound as Great Northern Train 4. Both operated daily between Chicago, St. Paul, Minneapolis, Spokane, Seattle, and Portland, with direct connections to and from

This advertisement from 1953 includes the *Western Star* as the sister streamliner to the *Empire Builder*. By now, the livery for both the FTA and F3A diesels included the Pullman Green along the full length of the tops of all units. *Author collection*

Tacoma, California, and Vancouver, British Columbia. They were listed in schedules and timetables as operating with lightweight streamlined equipment.

All accommodations on the *Empire Builder* were reserved at no extra fare. The observation car operated between Chicago and Seattle, and had buffet service and AM radio reception in the car. Standard sleepers offered seven of the latest types of Pullman accommodations, including drawing rooms, compartments, double bedrooms, roomettes, duplex roomettes, and lower and upper berths. Between Chicago and Seattle, there were four sleepers both westbound and eastbound. Between Chicago and Portland, there were two sleepers both westbound and eastbound

On the Mid-Century *Empire Builder*, passengers became "pardners" and were invited to "Ride the Ranch"—the G-Bar-N Ranch Car, that is. Comfort was corralled when the Great Northern rebranded its *Empire Builder* coffee shop in the early 1950s. To our smug twenty-first century sensibilities, "real Montana brands" and "Pinto pony furnishings" may seem kitschy, but when the Great Northern's management tried to get rid of the Ranch in 1955, a tidal wave of passenger complaints disabused them of this unconsidered move. Pardners continued to ride the Ranch until 1967. *Author collection*

Left: The two double-headed Class W-1 electrics that the Great Northern operated on the Cascade Division were the largest electric locomotives in the world in their day. Built by General Electric in June 1947, they were the only electric units delivered to the Great Northern in *Empire Builder* colors. They were retired in August 1956, and sadly both were scrapped. They would have been priceless museum objects today. *Author collection*

This Great Northern motive power group photo was taken at the railroad's big shops and roundhouse facility at Appleyard, near Wenatchee, Washington. We can see how the massive W-1 electric dwarfs other locomotives. In the center is an Electro-Motive Division FTA diesel, and on the right is an R-2 Class 2-8-8-2 steam locomotive. Ironically, the big electrics were phased out while the Great Northern was still running a few steam locomotives on its lines. *Author collection*

on the Spokane, Portland & Seattle Railway. Between Spokane and Portland, one sleeper contained six roomettes and three double bedrooms, as well as buffet-lounge facilities.

Advance reservations for Pullman accommodations could be made at any time prior to the scheduled departure. An exception was that seats for intermediate travel between any two stations west of Havre, or between any two stations east of Havre, could not be reserved until 24 hours prior to train departure time eastbound from Seattle-Portland or westbound from Chicago.

Streamlined Day Nite coaches on the *Empire Builder* offered reclining seats with leg rests that formed a couch for sleeping, as well as individual reading lights and pillows. All seats could be reserved in advance at no extra charge, but advance coach seat reservations had to be made so that definite coach seat assignment was obtained before departure. Seats could also be reserved for children under five years of age at no extra fare. Two lounges set aside in the women's Day Nite coaches had curtained dressing alcoves.

The *Empire Builder*'s extremely popular G-Bar-N Ranch coffee shop and lounge car was available for both coach and Pullman passengers. Counter and table service were available at what the Great Northern described as "economical prices." The club breakfasts were listed for 70 cents, 95 cents, and $1.35, depending upon what was chosen from a menu including fruits and fruit juices, cereal, eggs, toast, rolls, doughnuts, and beverages. Plate luncheons and dinners started at $1.25 and included soups, sandwiches, salads, desserts, and beverages. These were available throughout the day. The Ranch also boasted its AM radio reception.

Pulled by a motive power unit consisting of two F3A cab units and an F3B power unit, the *Empire Builder* makes its way through the canyon of the Middle Fork of the Flathead River between Red Eagle and Belton, Montana. The snow-capped Rockies of Glacier National Park are seen in the distance. *BNSF Archives*

A 10-car *Empire Builder* heads north out of Seattle along Puget Sound. After the Everett stop at 3:55 that afternoon, it will turn east toward the Cascade Tunnel. Arriving in Spokane at 10:45 that evening, it will receive additional cars that left Portland at 3:00 p.m. *Author collection*

EMPIRE
BUILDER

The distinctive *Empire Builder* neon is visible on the club car as the Mid-Century edition of the streamliner arrives at Seattle's King Street Station in 1953. The 1906 tower of the relatively quiet station is visible in the center. The building on the left is the Smith Tower. Completed in 1914, the 42-story structure was the fourth tallest building in the world, and the tallest outside New York, at the time. It remained the tallest in Seattle until the Space Needle was erected for the 1962 World's Fair. *Author collection*

In the dining car, a passenger could settle into a semiprivate dining section for a traditional Great Northern meal. Club breakfasts started at $1.00, plate luncheons at $1.50, and *table d'hote* luncheons at $1.90. Plate dinners started at $1.70 and *table d'hote* dinners were at $2.75. Passengers had their choice of one-hour dining periods beginning at 5:00 p.m., and the passenger representative on the train made arrangements for dinner reservations. To get an approximation of these prices in today's dollars, divide the prices by 16 percent. Breakfast would start at $6.25, and the *table d'hote* dinners would begin at just over $17.

The *Western Star* offered standard sleeping cars with deluxe Pullman accommodations between Chicago and Seattle. One car contained four sections, eight duplex roomettes, and four double bedrooms. Two *Western Star* cars contained 16 duplex roomettes and 4 double bedrooms. A fourth car contained a drawing room, two double bedrooms, and observation, lounge, and buffet areas. The double bedrooms were connecting rooms and were often sold *en suite* at the drawing room rate. Between Chicago and Portland, one car contained four sections, eight duplex

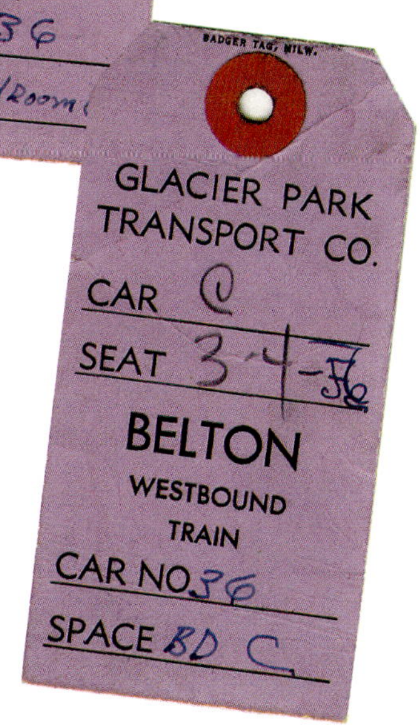

In the summer of 1951, Mr. and Mrs. Clyde Miller and their son Robert booked a bedroom compartment in Pullman Car No. 36 and travelled west from Chicago on the Great Northern. They stopped at Belton to tour Glacier National Park, and departed Belton for Seattle on July 26. On August 2, they left Seattle to return to Chicago. *Author collection*

This Great Northern timetable covered the schedule for the summer of 1952. The *Empire Builder* and the *Western Star* were the featured trains, and the two nearly identical F7A diesels subliminally suggested that the two trains were equals, even if the *Western Star* did take longer and make more stops between Chicago and Seattle. *Author collection*

Opposite: Sister streamliner to the *Empire Builder*, the *Western Star* was used during the 1950s to make the Great Northern's stops at Belton and East Glacier, serving the Glacier National Park trade between June 15 and September 10. Without those stops, which tended to be long, the *Empire Builder* offered a faster schedule between Chicago and Seattle. The painting depicts No. 365C, a F7A that was built in October 1950. *Author collection*

roomettes, and four double bedrooms. The Day-Night coaches on the *Western Star* offered the same amenities as those on the *Empire Builder*.

The *Western Star's* coffee shop, though not branded as G-Bar-N, offered meals at the same prices. The same was true for the *Western Star* dining car. Dinner reservations were offered during the June 15 to September 10 summer season.

Other streamlined trains operating on the Great Northern in the 1950s included the *Red River*, which operated between St. Paul and Grand Forks, North Dakota, as train No. 11 westbound and as train No. 12 eastbound; as well as the three *Internationals* that made round trips between Seattle and Vancouver, British Columbia. These operated as Trains 356, 360, and 362 northbound, and as Trains 355, 357, and 361 southbound. Trains No. 5 and 6, the daily *Cascadian* between Spokane and Seattle, trains No. 7 and 8, and the *Winnipeg Limited* service between the Twin Cities and Winnipeg were not streamlined until later.

You'll talk for years about your Glacier Park vacation
How you explored Montana's Rocky Mountain magic in Glacier National Park—and discovered the secret of world-famous Trick Falls, one of America's wonders.
How you relaxed in Nature's own air-conditioning—and thrilled to Glacier's snow-capped peaks—right from the sun deck of your luxurious mountain hotel.
How you vacationed on the way—forgot travel worries on Great Northern's safe, luxurious Western Star—direct to Glacier Park through 'Vacationland, U.S.A.'
How you photographed and talked with real Blackfeet Indians who greeted you at the train in full ceremonial dress—part of Glacier's excitingly colorful atmosphere.
How you marveled at the view from Logan Pass—6664 feet high on the Continental Divide—high point on the breath-taking 'Going-to-the-Sun' Highway.
How you harmonized that night on the shore of Swiftcurrent Lake—and promised yourself you'd come back soon to glorious Glacier—where there's more to see and do.
See America First!
Go carefree, be car-free...
Go Great Northern Streamliners
LOGAN PASS
365 A
GREAT NORTHERN RAILWAY
For information on Glacier Park, Pacific Northwest or California, write P. G. Holmes, Passenger Traffic Manager, Great Northern Railway, Department G-24, St. Paul 1, Minnesota. Ask for literature about Western vacations.
WESTERN STAR
STOPS DAILY IN GLACIER PARK, JUNE 15 THROUGH SEPTEMBER 10

Equipped with its set of three dome cars, the *Empire Builder* takes a bend just east of Glacier National Park. Announced in 1953, the short domes made their debut in time for the summer of 1955. The longer-domed lounge cars joined the roster in October 1955.
Author collection

Prices for the Mid-Century *Empire Builder* varied. A first class fare from Chicago to Seattle sold for $75.06 one way or $115.00 round trip. Coach prices for the same route were $53.61 for one way or $82.00 for a round trip. If you were travelling from Chicago to Glacier Park and wanted to book Pullman sleeping car accommodations, you would add $15.40 for a standard lower berth. The round-trip first class fare over the entire *Empire Builder* route was the equivalent of more than $700 in turn of the century dollars.

On a typical trip on the Mid-Century *Empire Builder*, you would depart Chicago at 1:00 p.m., let's say on a Monday. You travel on the Chicago, Burlington & Quincy trackage non-stop to St. Paul, arriving at 7:45 p.m. Monday evening. Switching to Great Northern track, you depart St. Paul at 8:15 p.m. and stop in Minneapolis 30 minutes later. At 10:16 p.m., the *Empire Builder* reaches Willmar,

The westbound Mid-Century *Empire Builder* was captured during the summer of 1995 between Essex and Nyack, Montana. The peaks within Glacier National Park in the background are, from left, Lone Walker Mountain, Caper Peak, Battlement Mountain, and Mount St. Nicholas. *Courtesy of W. J. Yenne*

Minnesota, and at 12:05 a.m. on Tuesday, you'd probably doze off as the train makes its whistle stop in Breckenridge, Minnesota.

The *Empire Builder* crosses the North Dakota line at Fargo at 1:15 a.m. and continues across most of the state in the dark. At New Rockford, few people are awake for the 3:08 a.m. stop, but people might be stirring as the train leaves Minot at 4:55 a.m. The sun would be coming up as the *Empire Builder* reaches Williston, North Dakota, at 7:20 a.m. Although the change from Central Time to Mountain Time would be at the Montana border, 20 miles west of Williston, the conductor sets his watch back to 6:20 a.m. in Williston.

The first Montana stop for the *Empire Builder* would be at Glasgow at 9:10 a.m., just in time for a late breakfast. The second stop in the vast wide-openness of Montana's highline would be Havre at 12:10 p.m., which was time to head down to the G-Bar-N Ranch for an early lunch. This stop takes you past the Great Northern's big Diesel Shops where maintenance on the F7 units is carried out.

How could anyone resist the *Empire Builder* and the Great Dome lounge cars after looking at an advertisement such as this? Unfortunately, the artist took a great deal of license in this spectacular painting because there is no place on the "Route of the *Empire Builder*" that looks like this. Places within Glacier National Park sort of look like this, but no rails are there. The Great Northern boasted that each *Empire Builder* had 147 seats beneath the domes, although not all the seats are taken in this illustration. *Author collection*

DOMES
EMPIRE BUILDER
NOW! FASTEST TRAIN CHICAGO TO SEATTLE!
BUILDER
BETWEEN CHICAGO·TWIN CITIES·SPOKANE·SEATTLE·PORTLAND
GREAT NORTHERN
VANCOUVER
WINNIPEG
EVERETT
SEATTLE
TACOMA
WENATCHEE
SPOKANE
MINOT
GRAND FORKS
DULUTH
SUPERIOR
GREAT FALLS
FARGO
ST. PAUL
MINNEAPOLIS
PORTLAND
HELENA
BILLINGS
BUTTE
CHICAGO
TO CALIFORNIA
GO THE GREAT DOME ROUTE CONNECTIONS TO AND FROM CALIFORNIA
GREAT NORTHERN RAILWAY

This is what it looks like inside the *Empire Builder* Great Dome lounge car. The plush seats guaranteed a comfortable ride, and the virtually limitless windows guaranteed a sensational view as the streamliner zipped across the continent. The modern Amtrak Superliners afford a reasonable facsimile of the experience, but there is nothing like a Budd car. Five of the original six still exist in the twenty-first century. *BNSF Archives*

The *Empire Builder's* Montana stops through the early afternoon come in rapid succession. Chester is at 1:18 p.m., followed by Shelby at 2:10 p.m. and Cut Bank at 2:43 p.m. This afternoon is time to break out the camera, as the *Empire Builder* climbs Marias Pass and hugs the southern periphery of Glacier National Park. Evening is upon you as the train makes its 6:05 p.m. stop in Whitefish, now one of Montana's most important ski resort areas.

Night has fallen by 9:10 p.m. as the *Empire Builder* passes through the last Montana stop at Troy and into the Pacific Time Zone at the Idaho border. It is 11:30 p.m. Pacific. Three hours and 20 minutes out of Troy, the train reaches Spokane where the cars aboard the *Empire Builder* are efficiently shuffled to Spokane, Portland & Seattle Rail-way trackage for the trip to Portland, and the *Empire Builder* continues on to Seattle.

The *Empire Builder* is scheduled to depart Spokane at 11:59 p.m., one minute before Wednesday begins. At 2:12 a.m. and at 3:35 a.m., most passengers are snoring through their second night on the *Empire Builder* as the train makes its dead-of-night stops at Ephrata and Wenatchee. Until 1956, the *Empire Builder*

This cutaway view of the *Empire Builder* Great Dome lounge car Glacier View takes us inside for just a hint of the fun that was available in the golden age of American streamliners. *Author collection*

switched motive power at Wenatchee for the 75-mile run to Skykomish by way of the Cascade Tunnel. The Electro-Motive Division F7 equipment is detached to pick up an eastbound *Empire Builder*, and a General Electric Class W-1 electric locomotive takes over. By 5:49 a.m., most passengers are barely awake as the big W-1 hands the *Empire Builder* off to another F7 diesel for the last leg of the journey.

The *Empire Builder* reaches Everett at 7:02 a.m. in time to make the picturesque run along Puget Sound in daylight. Less than an hour later, at 8:00 a.m. sharp on Wednesday morning, the *Empire Builder* pulls into King Street Station in Seattle. Those not debarking here in the Emerald City may remain on the train for the last short run to Tacoma, where the *Empire Builder* will terminate its transcontinental run at 9:12 a.m.

For comparison purposes, let's return to Chicago by way of the Great Northern's *Western Star*. From Seattle's King Street Station, we depart at 10:15 p.m. on Monday, while the *Empire Builder* had already departed at 3:00 that afternoon. This sends the *Western Star* across Washington State in the dark, while the *Empire Builder* makes the trip in the evening. The *Empire Builder* will reach Spokane at 10:45 p.m. Monday, just a half hour after the *Western Star* pulls out of King Street.

On our eastbound *Western Star* return, we arrive in Everett at 11:14 p.m., and by 12:32 a.m. on Tuesday, we are at Skykomish for the transition to electric motive power. We doze off as the *Western Star* glides through the Cascade Tunnel and don't even

The number of upper and lower berths on the Mid-Century *Empire Builder* was officially described as limited. Foam mattresses were offered. *Author collection*

The Duplex Roomettes on the Mid-Century *Empire Builder*, like those on the earlier New *Empire Builder*, were offered at 10 percent over the cost of lower berth. *Author collection*

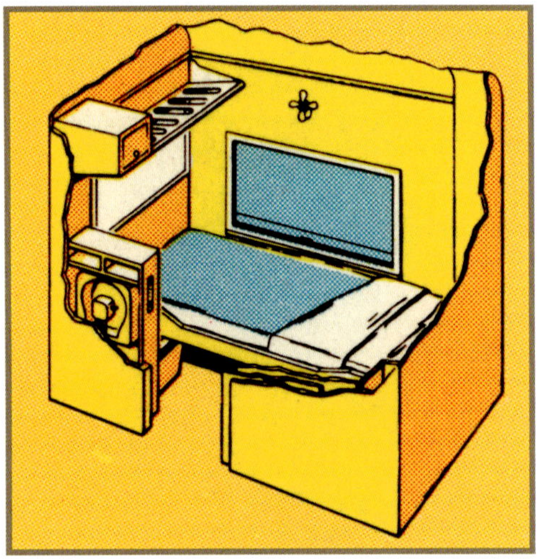

With private toilet facilities, the Roomette on the Mid-Century *Empire Builder* was called "a self-contained home on wheels." *Author collection*

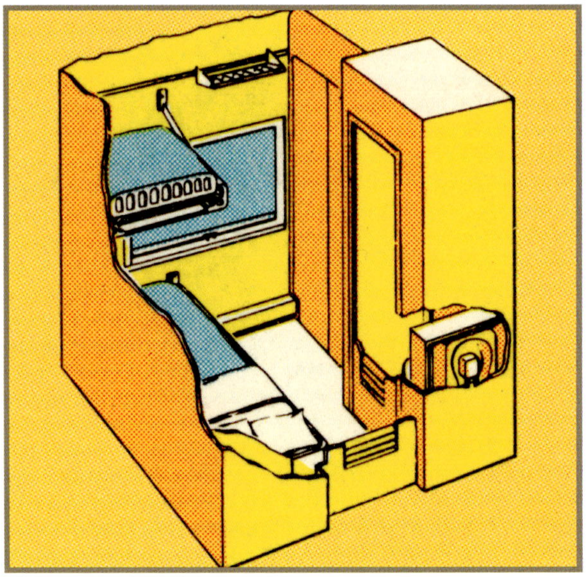

The Mid-Century *Empire Builder* offered double bedrooms and singles for two people travelling together. The sofa made into one bed, and the second pulled down from above. *Author collection*

Compartments on the Mid-Century *Empire Builder* had a sofa-seat that became a bed, and there was room enough for an extra chair. The toilet was enclosed. *Author collection*

The epitome of accommodation on the Mid-Century *Empire Builder* was the compartment-bedroom suite, which was a spacious room by day and two rooms by night. As with other rooms available in the 1960s, it was the same configuration offered in the 1947 New *Empire Builder*. *Author collection*

wake up as the train reaches Wenatchee at 2:50 a.m. and the F7 units are attached. The Ephrata stop comes at 4:16 a.m., and we are in Spokane at 6:50 a.m. as the eastern horizon grows light with the dawn. The cars that came up through the Columbia Gorge from Portland on the Spokane, Portland & Seattle Railway tracks are attached to the *Western Star* at Spokane. This complex procedure is second nature for the yard crews. It takes less than an hour and we are underway at 7:20 a.m.

It's time for our first breakfast aboard the eastbound *Western Star*, as it passes through Idaho into Montana. We arrive in Troy at 10:35 a.m., and leave five minutes later at 11:40 a.m. as the conductor adjusts his watch to the Mountain Time Zone. The *Empire Builder* travelling through before us had passed this way at 3:40 a.m. as most passengers were sound asleep.

Stylized illustrations were a feature of this widely used 1965 advertisement for the *Empire Builder*. Built 15 years earlier, Locomotive No. 365-A was an F7A that had been featured in previous advertising and other illustration styles for more than a decade. Smoking in the coach or dining car was still considered to be acceptable and worthy of being advertised. Today it is explicitly forbidden on the Amtrak *Empire Builder*. *Author collection*

The *Western Star* reaches Whitefish at 2:40 p.m. and Columbia Falls just 12 minutes later. From here, we pass through Bad Rock Canyon and past the mouth of the South Fork of the Flathead River on our final dash to the western entrance to Glacier National Park. We arrive at Belton at 3:18 p.m., where passengers detrain to board the bright red Glacier Park Company Jammer buses for their trip into the park. On our right are the Belton Chalets, which were sold off as excess by the Great Northern subsidiary. On our left is the

Empire Builder Dining Car Recipes:
Great Northern Lemon Pie

(As baked by *Empire Builder* Chef Fred Tobiska)

Mix yolks of 20 eggs, one pound sugar, and the juice and grated rind of eight lemons. Cook all over slow fire until it thickens. Remove from fire and stir in whites of 10 eggs, beaten very hard. Pour into pie plates lined with pie dough and bake in a moderate oven for 25 minutes.

town of West Glacier and the park boundary. The town, like the Great Northern train station, used to be called Belton, but on October 1, 1949, the promoters of tourism changed the name to mirror the town of East Glacier on the other side of the Continental Divide.

Our passage along the 60 miles of the southern edge of Glacier National Park comes between 3:18 p.m. and 5:01 p.m. on Tuesday. For travellers aboard the eastbound *Empire Builder* today, those miles are passed during breakfast, between 7:00 and 9:00 a.m. As we gaze at the park's dramatic scenery, we pass the westbound *Empire Builder*.

At 5:01 in the evening, the *Western Star* makes its stop at East Glacier, where the station is just a short stroll from the immense Glacier Park Lodge, with the cluster of Blackfeet teepees on the broad front lawn. The *Western Star* travellers coming from the east arrived today at 12:55 p.m., just in time for a late lunch in the dining room at the lodge, with its spectacular view of the nearby front range of the Rocky Mountains.

The East Glacier stop, like the one at Belton, occurs only between June 15 and September 10. When the snow comes, the Glacier National Park will hibernate for most of the year. The Mid-Century *Empire Builder* will not make this stop at all. The *Empire Builder* was once the only train to make this stop, and as the *Western Star* faded into history, the Amtrak *Empire Builder* is the only train to make this stop.

The *Western Star* reaches Cut Bank, Montana, at 6:06 p.m. and Shelby 34 minutes later. Another major difference between the *Western Star* and the Mid-Century *Empire Builder* comes into play. While the *Empire Builder* will head straight across the Great Plains to the Twin Cities, the *Western Star* will pause to make a side trip south to the city of Great Falls. The *Western Star* arrives in Great Falls at 9:20 p.m., turns around, and departs at 9:35 p.m.

Back on the Great Northern mainline, the *Western Star* will pass by the huge diesel maintenance base at Havre at 12:30 a.m. on Wednesday. By now, the *Empire Builder*, which left Seattle a little more than seven hours ahead of us, is 13 hours and 10 minutes ahead and already past Grand Forks, North Dakota.

The *Western Star* reaches Glasgow at 3:45 a.m.; the only passengers awake are those who wish to detrain here.

We arrive in Williston, North Dakota, at 6:40 a.m. and leave five minutes later at 7:45—again the conductor changes his watch as we mourn the loss of an hour to entering the Central Time Zone. It's time for breakfast as the *Western Star* hurtles toward its 10:25 a.m. stop in Minot.

At 2:45 p.m., the *Western Star* is in Grand Forks, and by 4:40 p.m. we are approaching the Minnesota line as we stop at Fargo. As we make the Breckenridge, Minnesota, stop at 5:45 p.m., it's time for our last dinner onboard this Great Northern adventure. At 7:55 p.m., the train stops at Willmar, and we head for the club car to scare up a card game.

This timetable covering the period from October 30, 1966, through April 29, 1967, included the last winter the *Empire Builder* ran in the color scheme of Omaha Orange and Pullman Green. It was also the last winter the author lived within earshot of the mainline of the Great Northern. *Author collection*

With a red light and the neon logo illuminated at the end of the observation car, the *Empire Builder* passes through Wenatchee, circa 1964. During the mid-1960s, the streamliner arrived here at 3:10 a.m. westbound and at 7:10 p.m. eastbound. *Gil Hulin*

The *Western Star* arrives in Minneapolis at 9:55 p.m., and is in St. Paul by 10:30 p.m. The *Empire Builder*, which departed with its seven hour head start was in Minneapolis at 6:30 a.m. this morning, and in St. Paul at 7:00. We begin our last night on the *Western Star* as the train shifts from the main line of the Great Northern to the tracks of the Chicago, Burlington & Quincy. We pull out of St. Paul at 11:15 p.m. on Wednesday, with no further stops between here and the Windy City. At 7:55 a.m. on Thursday morning, we are just finishing our coffee as the streamliner pulls into Chicago's Union Station. The next *Western Star* westbound departure will be at 11:15 tonight, while the next *Empire Builder* will pull out for Seattle at 1:00 this afternoon.

This trip was a manifestation of the vastness of the continent. We have seen the endless prairies where the buffalo once roamed. We have seen the land of the Blackfeet, recently a nomadic stone-age people, who now spend their summers informing tourists of their culture at the Glacier Park Lodge. We have seen the Rocky Mountains, with their forests and the surging rivers. We have seen the Great Plains of central Washington, and we have traveled through the towering Cascades by way of the longest tunnel on the continent. We have seen Puget Sound, with its countless islands, and Seattle, the metropolis of the Pacific Northwest.

The *Empire Builder*, and its sister train, the *Western Star*, were more than streamliners. They were, and the *Empire Builder* still is, windows on a great land.

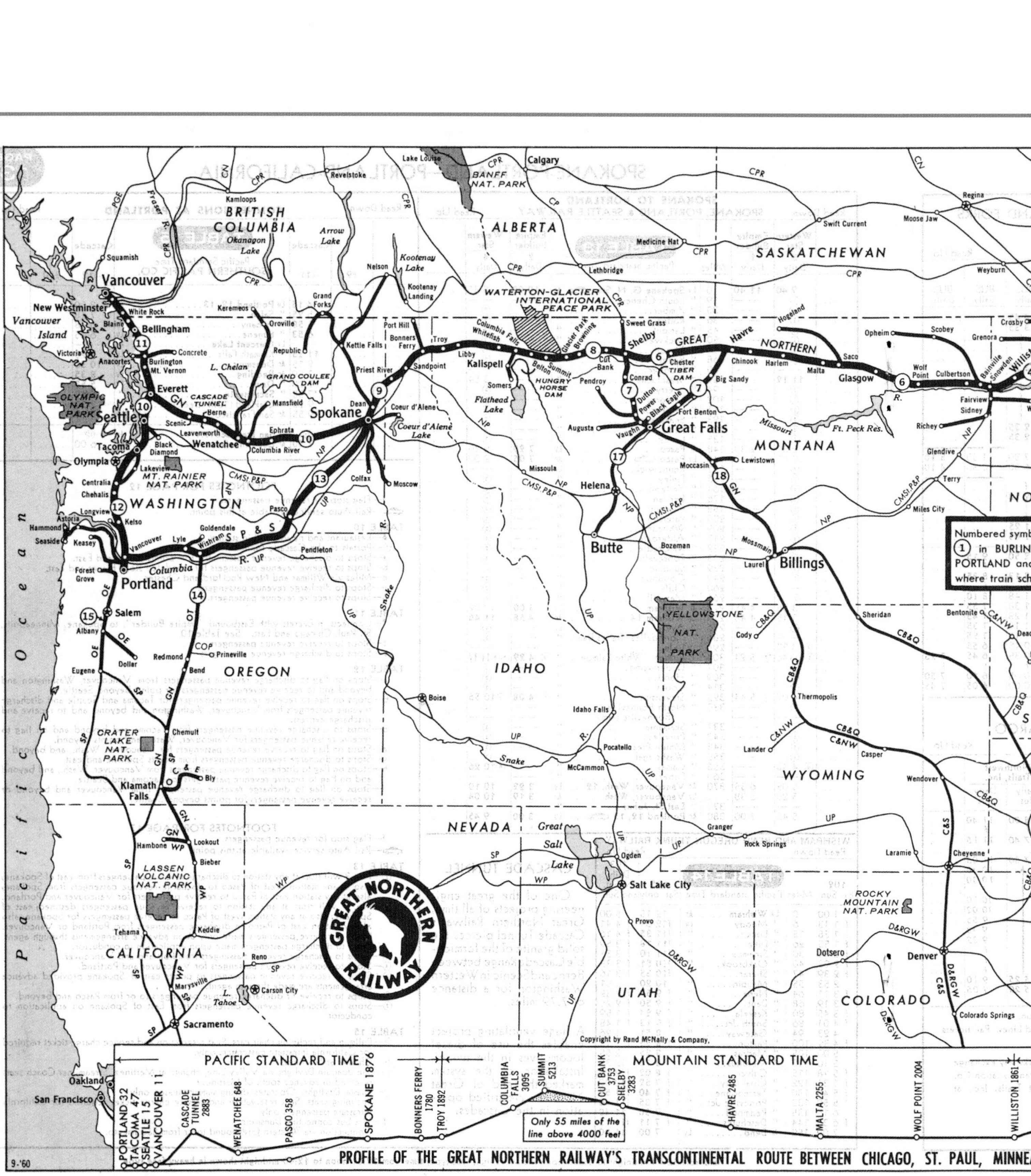
BRITISH COLUMBIA
ALBERTA
SASKATCHEWAN
WASHINGTON
OREGON
IDAHO
MONTANA
WYOMING
NEVADA
UTAH
COLORADO
CALIFORNIA
Pacific Ocean
Vancouver
New Westminster
Vancouver Island
Victoria
Bellingham
Everett
Seattle
Tacoma
Olympia
Spokane
Wenatchee
Portland
Salem
Klamath Falls
Sacramento
Oakland
San Francisco
Calgary
BANFF NAT. PARK
WATERTON-GLACIER INTERNATIONAL PEACE PARK
Kalispell
Whitefish
Shelby
Havre
Glasgow
Great Falls
Helena
Butte
Billings
Lewistown
Williston
Boise
Idaho Falls
Pocatello
Ogden
Salt Lake City
Denver
Cheyenne
YELLOWSTONE NAT. PARK
OLYMPIC NAT. PARK
MT. RAINIER NAT. PARK
CRATER LAKE NAT. PARK
LASSEN VOLCANIC NAT. PARK
ROCKY MOUNTAIN NAT. PARK
GREAT NORTHERN
Columbia River
Missouri R.
Snake R.
Great Salt Lake
CASCADE TUNNEL
GRAND COULEE DAM
HUNGRY HORSE DAM
TIBER DAM
Ft. Peck Res.
Numbered symb
1 in BURLING
PORTLAND and
where train sche
GREAT NORTHERN RAILWAY
Copyright by Rand McNally & Company.
PACIFIC STANDARD TIME
MOUNTAIN STANDARD TIME
PORTLAND 32
TACOMA 47
SEATTLE 15
VANCOUVER 11
CASCADE TUNNEL 2883
WENATCHEE 648
PASCO 358
SPOKANE 1876
BONNERS FERRY 1780
TROY 1892
COLUMBIA FALLS 3095
SUMMIT 5213
CUT BANK 3753
SHELBY 3283
HAVRE 2485
MALTA 2255
WOLF POINT 2004
WILLISTON 1861
Only 55 miles of the line above 4000 feet
PROFILE OF THE GREAT NORTHERN RAILWAY'S TRANSCONTINENTAL ROUTE BETWEEN CHICAGO, ST. PAUL, MINNEA
9-'60

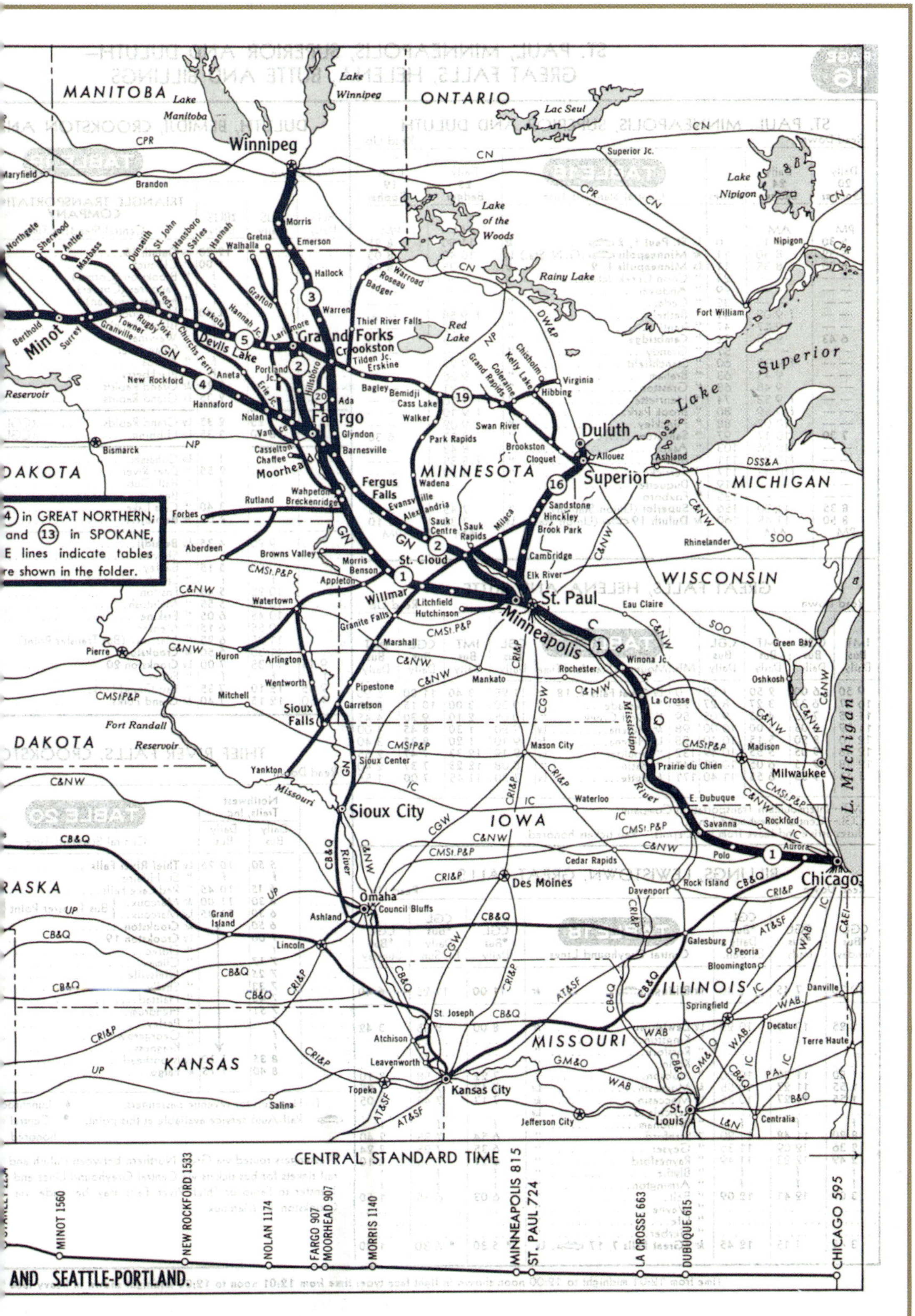

This map traces the route of the Empire Builder on the main line of the Great Northern, as well as the numerous connecting trains belonging to both the Great Northern and cooperating roads. Across the bottom of the map is a cross section of the Empire Builder, showing the elevations of points on the main line from Seattle to Chicago. The apex was Montana's Marias Pass. *Author collection*

333
333

Six

From Big Sky Blue to Cascade Green

As the *Empire Builder* enjoyed its golden age, a new paradigm was emerging. This was the dawn of the family road trip. While the 1950s saw record numbers of people taking vacations by rail, the era also saw the advent of one of the largest engineering efforts in human history—the construction of the U.S. Interstate Highway System. It was also an era when passenger air travel was coming of age. In the years immediately after World War II, the Great Northern had rapidly lost market share to private automobiles on its shorter passenger runs. As air travel matured, especially with the introduction of jetliners in the late 1950s, the railroads lost essentially all of their long distance business travellers.

This left long-haul vacation traffic, an area where the Great Northern clearly excelled. However, even here, the times were changing. Before World War II, most visitors to Glacier National Park had travelled on the *Empire Builder*. After the war, the tables had turned. By the end of the 1950s, only a small sliver of the park's visitors arrived on the Great Northern. This was despite the fact that interstate highways across Montana were among the last completed, and that no east–west interstate was built within 150 miles of the park.

It was not just the passenger business nor the Great Northern; by the 1960s, the railroad business in general was going through a serious slump. The Interstate Highway System carried family station wagons and a burgeoning volume of long-haul trucking. This hurt the freight business of the railroads. It was harder east of Chicago. Many of the once great eastern roads were teetering on the edge of collapse. In the West, where the scale of the vast land was more suited to railroads, conditions continued to keep the companies in business.

The *Empire Builder* in Big Sky Blue makes the turn at Pinnacle, Montana, across the river from Glacier National Park, in September 1967. The *Empire Builder* was still running with its full complement of four dome cars. Motive power is an Electro-Motive Division SDP45 that had been in service with the Great Northern for less than a month when this picture was taken. No. 333 was the last passenger locomotive ever delivered to the Great Northern. *BNSF Archives*

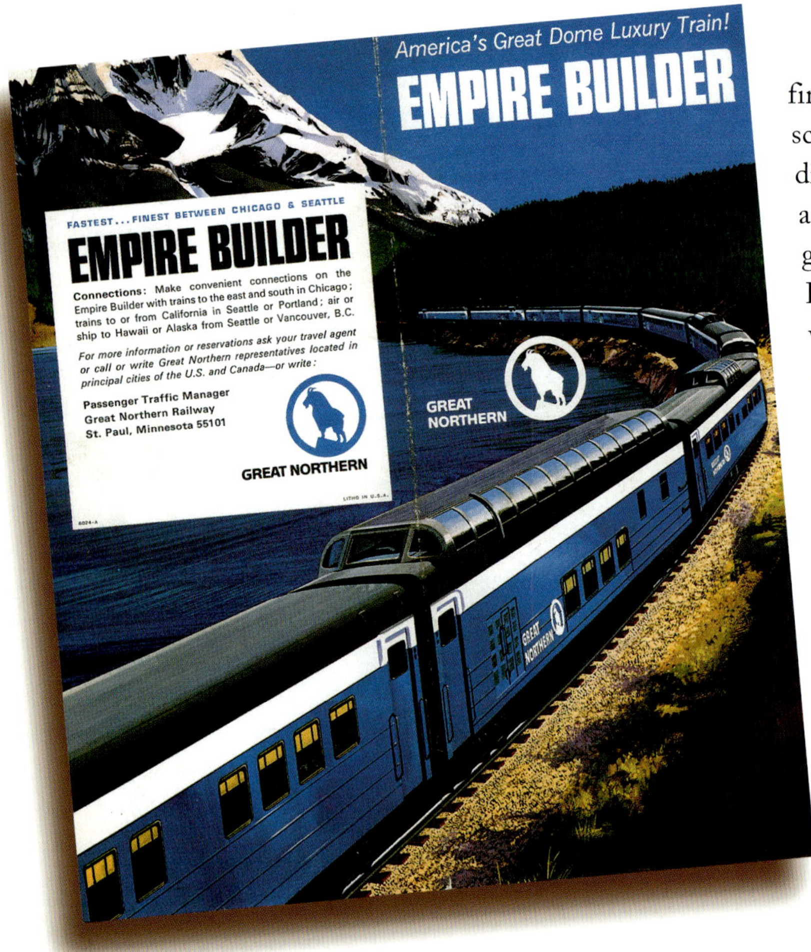

One of the last brochures produced by the Great Northern for *Empire Builder*, this marketing piece featured the simplified Rocky mascot and an illustration of the streamliner in Big Sky Blue with a pair of SPD45s on the front. Of course, the Rocky Mountains were still a requisite part of the image. *Author collection*

In 1962, the Great Northern made the first change to the *Empire Builder* color scheme since the introduction of the F7 diesel units a decade earlier. Intended to save a day of painting time, the stripe of metallic gold paint between the Omaha Orange and Pullman Green was omitted. The change was applicable to all Great Northern diesels, including both passenger and freight equipment.

Meanwhile, the Great Northern was compelled to make a major investment in infrastructure. In the spring of 1966, the first phase of construction began on the giant $352-million Libby Dam project in northwest Montana. Damming the Kootenai River a short distance above Libby created a 90-mile long reservoir that extended into Canada. The Great Northern's main line was inundated for 48 miles, and its relocation required 59 miles of new line and the construction of the seven-mile Flathead Tunnel, which became operational in 1970. The new line was the largest railroad construction project of its decade in the United States and the most extensive single undertaking on the Great Northern in 36 years. Meanwhile, the Great Northern itself had reached an important milestone. In October 1965, the company officially became a billion-dollar enterprise. The principal commodities in its diversified traffic mix at that time were, in order of importance, grain and grain products, lumber and wood products, and iron ore. Passengers had never represented more than a small proportion, and that proportion had been declining since World War II.

By this time, the Great Northern's F units had been in service for more than a decade and the company was ready to order new equipment. In May 1966, the Electro-Motive Division rolled out six new diesels for the Great Northern, and the last locomotives were delivered in the *Empire Builder* paint scheme. Lacking the attractive streamlined styling of the earlier E and F units, these new locomotives were all business. The six-axle, C-C configured Class SDP40 diesels delivered 3,000 horsepower. The six SDP40s were augmented by eight SDP45 units that were built by the Electro-Motive Division in June and August 1967. They were similar in appearance to the SDP40 units, but had more power (3,600 horsepower each).

The arrival of the SDP45 units coincided with the Great Northern's last change in livery. In 1967, the Great Northern adopted a comprehensive corporate

identification program recommended by the internationally known design firm of Lippincott & Marguiles. A new corporate color, Big Sky Blue, was officially introduced on May 11, and standards for every conceivable use of the trademark and color were adopted by the Great Northern.

Since the early 1960s, the term "Big Sky" referred to the official Montana state slogan. The term is a reference to the title of A. B. Guthrie's 1947 novel, which was set in Montana. Before that, Montana was proudly identified as the "Treasure State" because of the riches that spilled forth from the mines at Butte. Jim Hill would probably have preferred to retain the former appellation, for he certainly recalled the glory days when tons upon tons of copper ore made Butte the "Richest Hill on Earth." Even if a great deal of that ore went out from Butte on roads other than the Great Northern, this image would have been more to his liking.

The old Omaha Orange and Pullman Green *Empire Builder* paint scheme was retired in 1967, and the entire Great Northern fleet, including locomotives, rolling stock, and passenger and freight equipment, was repainted in Big Sky Blue. In the locomotives and passenger cars, the bright blue predominated, but the roofs were black and there was a broad white band near the tops of the sides. The mountain goat logo was retained, but "Rocky" was simplified and rendered in silhouette.

Even as the new livery was seen across the northern tier of the United States from the Pacific Northwest to the northern plains, the Great Northern was involved in an effort to make both itself and the new paint a

Upper left: These post-1967 *Empire Builder* marketing materials included a photo from the Ranch Car that featured a lady wearing that most fashionable of colors—Big Sky Blue. The map linked the *International* route between Seattle and Vancouver, British Columbia, to the *Empire Builder*. The photo of the waiter in the lower left was one of the most widely used images in *Empire Builder* materials during the final decade of the Great Northern. *Author collection*

Above: Marketing for the final Great Northern *Empire Builder* in the late 1960s focused on the same theme that had been important for more than a dozen years—the dome cars, especially the Great Dome lounge car. *Author collection*

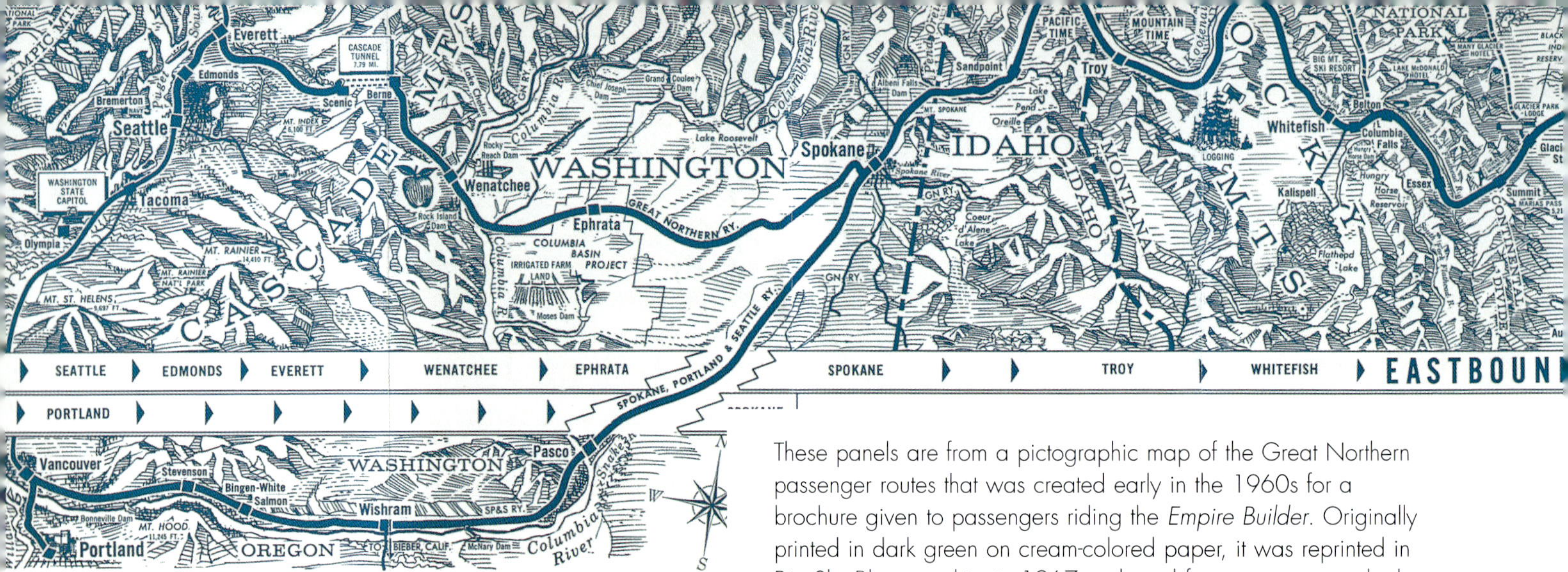

These panels are from a pictographic map of the Great Northern passenger routes that was created early in the 1960s for a brochure given to passengers riding the *Empire Builder*. Originally printed in dark green on cream-colored paper, it was reprinted in Big Sky Blue on white in 1967 and used for passengers on both the *Empire Builder* and the *Western Star*. *Author collection*

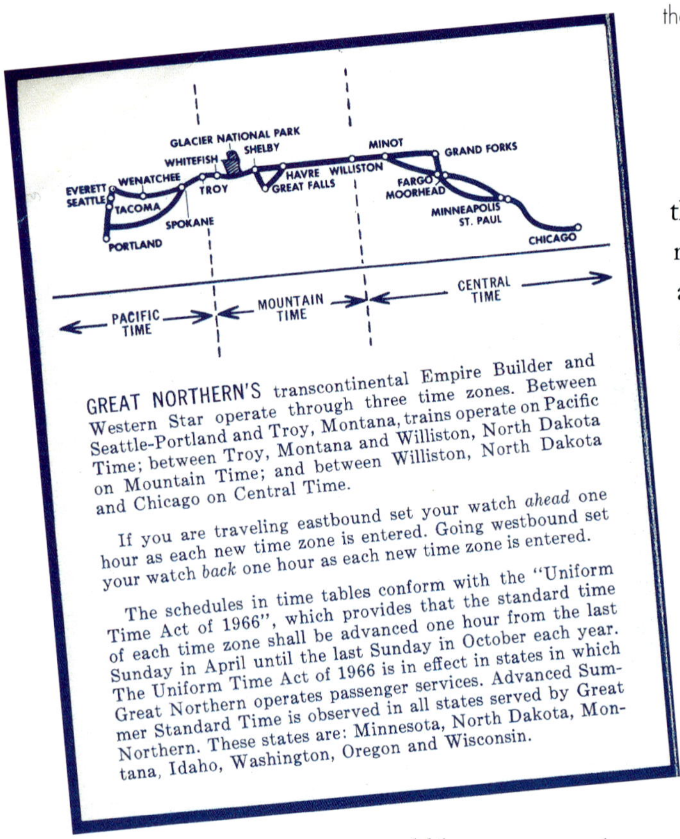

GREAT NORTHERN'S transcontinental Empire Builder and Western Star operate through three time zones. Between Seattle-Portland and Troy, Montana, trains operate on Pacific Time; between Troy, Montana and Williston, North Dakota on Mountain Time; and between Williston, North Dakota and Chicago on Central Time.

If you are traveling eastbound set your watch *ahead* one hour as each new time zone is entered. Going westbound set your watch *back* one hour as each new time zone is entered.

The schedules in time tables conform with the "Uniform Time Act of 1966", which provides that the standard time of each time zone shall be advanced one hour from the last Sunday in April until the last Sunday in October each year. The Uniform Time Act of 1966 is in effect in states in which Great Northern operates passenger services. Advanced Summer Standard Time is observed in all states served by Great Northern. These states are: Minnesota, North Dakota, Montana, Idaho, Washington, Oregon and Wisconsin.

thing of the past. In 1893 and 1901, Hill had tried to merge the Great Northern with the Northern Pacific and the Chicago, Burlington & Quincy. The federal government denied both of Hill's attempts to create such a monopoly. The concept was revisited unsuccessfully in 1927.

As the two roads went their separate ways through most of the twentieth century, Jim Hill's notion that the Great Northern and the Northern Pacific should someday be one was never ever really forgotten. The irony of the fact that executives of the two companies occupied opposite sides of the same venerable stone building in St. Paul was not lost. In fact, the two roads were really more cooperative than competitive. Their respective main lines were, for the most part, far separated. Together, they would be more complementary than redundant.

Even as the Great Northern presided over the golden age of the Mid-Century *Empire Builder*, President John Budd and Robert MacFarlane, his counterpart at the Northern Pacific, chatted informally in 1955.

In January 1956, the Great Northern Board of Directors went so far as to officially authorize an exploratory analysis of a possible merger. The Northern Pacific did the same. Bankers studied the potential merger from one angle, and engineers and economists examined it from their point of view. It took four years for the two companies to finally agree to a one-for-one exchange of shares. However, this was merely one tiny step. Nothing would be allowed to go forward without the acquiescence of the federal government's all-powerful Interstate Commerce Commission.

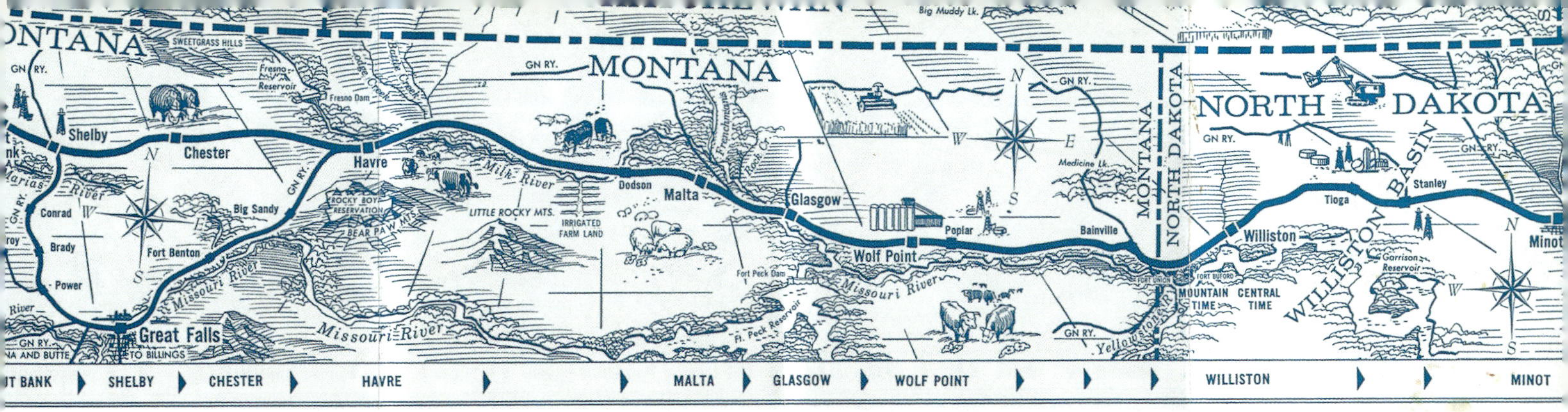

In the 1960s, as the fortunes of railroads throughout the nation were in decline, mergers now seemed to be not a matter of empire-building greed, but a key to survival. In the East, the New York Central and the Pennsylvania Railroad, once powerful rivals, fell into one another's arms. The Chesapeake & Ohio merged with rival Baltimore & Ohio. The Interstate Commerce Commission blessed these marriages because the roads involved were in desperate straights economically. The Great Northern and the Northern Pacific were very solvent.

In February 1961, the parties that Jim Hill had tried to make into one entity six decades earlier submitted their plan to the omnipotent lords of the Interstate Commerce Commission. The two Northerns planned to join and take the Chicago, Burlington & Quincy into the marriage bed with them. The new road would be called the Great Northern Pacific & Burlington Lines.

From October 1961 to August 1964, the Interstate Commerce Commission's man on the case, Robert Murphy, held hearings, heard testimony, studied exhibits, and pondered all the pros and cons. When stacked on a board room table, the transcript of the first round of Murphy's investigation was 60 inches high. When it was all over, Murphy gave the merger a thumbs up and observed that it would "promote the public interest by enabling the new company to provide more efficient and economical service."

This Electro-Motive Division GP7 road switcher was built for the Great Northern in 1950 and originally numbered as 620. Upon its takeover by Burlington Northern in 1970, it was renumbered as 1520, but the new owner retained the Big Sky Blue paint scheme. The locomotive was rebuilt in 1967 with the lowered nose and was retrofitted as a GP10 unit in 1975. *Author collection*

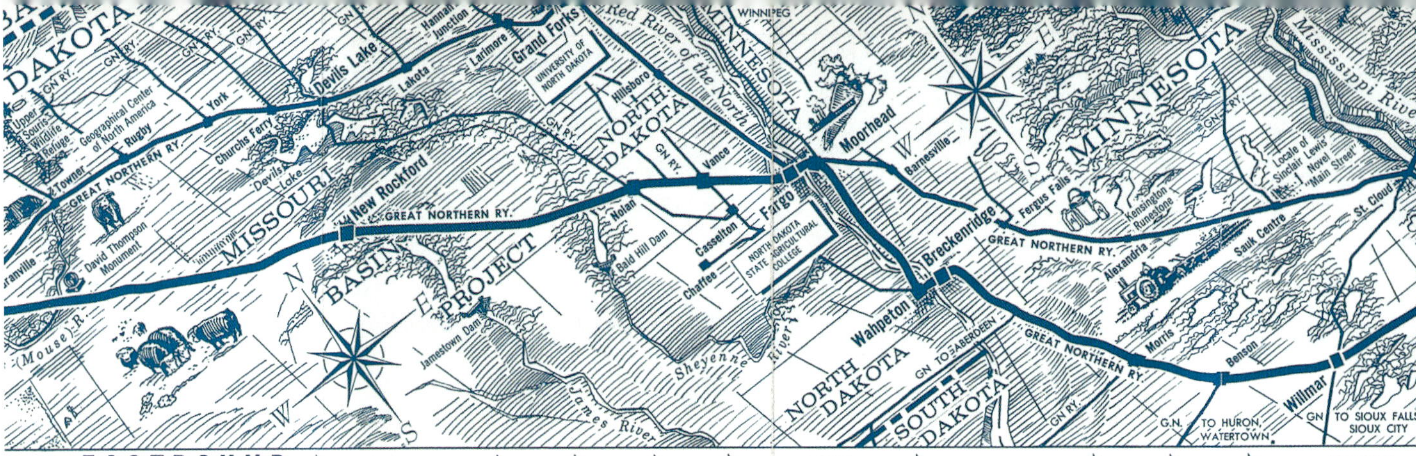

That should have been that, but the politicians disagreed. Neither Montana Senator Mike Mansfield, the Senate Majority Leader, nor Attorney General Robert F. Kennedy liked the notion of unifying the Great Northern and the Northern Pacific. Apparently allowing Pennsylvania and the New York Central to become Penn Central was alright, but a merger was not right for the Northerns.

In April 1966, two years after Robert Murphy issued his report, the Interstate Commerce Commission finally voted on the merger question. Despite Murphy's recommendation, the proposal lost by one vote. The Northerns went to work on the opposition and placated the unions and local politicians. Finally, in November 1967, half a year after the Great Northern repainted its fleet in Big Sky Blue, the Northerns were back before the Interstate Commerce Commission. This time, they won approval for the merger by a wide margin.

The approval brought an onslaught of complaints from politicians and rival railroads, and the frightened commissioners agreed to delay the effective date of the merger. Legal challenges to the merger went all the way to the U.S. Supreme Court, where the justices decreed in December 1968 to postpone the unification indefinitely. For more than a year, the case was argued in the high court, until February 1970 when the Supreme Court voted unanimously to remove the road block once and for all.

On March 2, 1970, it finally became official. Stationary had been printed and a new paint color was chosen. The Great Northern had merged with the Chicago, Burlington & Quincy Railroad and the Northern Pacific Railway to form the Burlington Northern Railroad. Also included in the merger was the Spokane, Portland & Seattle Railway, which was jointly owned by the two Northerns. In 1980, the St. Louis/San Francisco Railway, the "Frisco," was acquired and merged into the Burlington Northern.

After just three years, Big Sky Blue was phased out in favor of the new Cascade Green color scheme. The locomotives of the initial four components of the new Burlington Northern were painted Cascade Green, but the rolling stock generally remained the same. Big Sky Blue boxcars continued to be seen on the nation's railroads for decades after the Great Northern had ceased to exist.

At the time of the 1970 merger, the Great Northern Railway was, by a narrow margin, the second largest component of the new conglomerate. It had served a vast, diversified, and productive region comprised of the upper Midwest and the

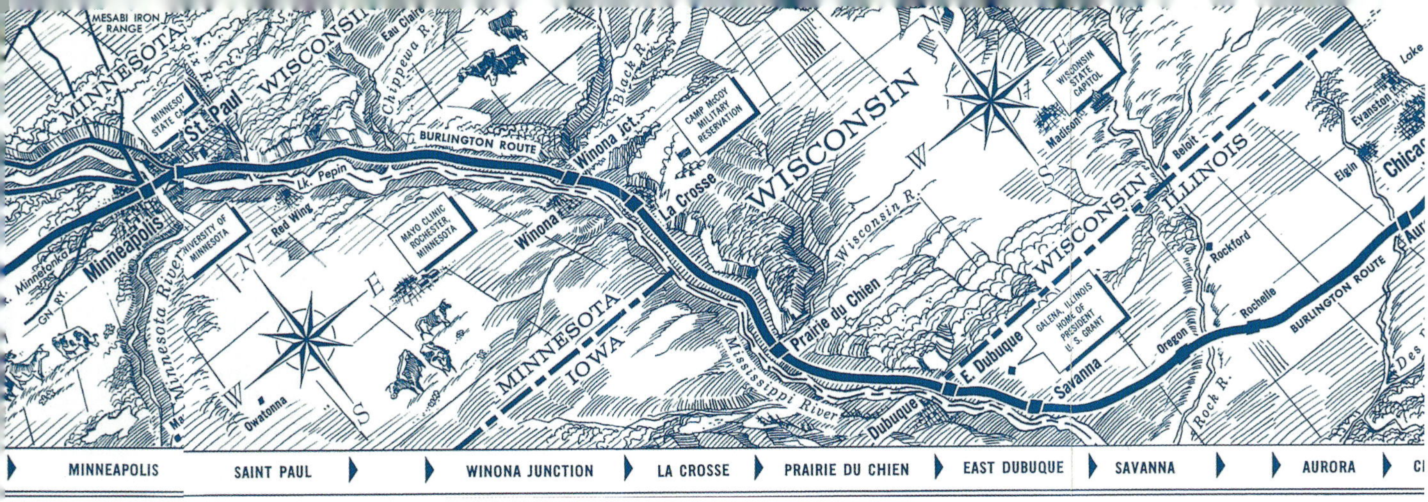

Northwest. On a system 8,277 miles in length (compared to 8,430 for the Chicago, Burlington & Quincy), its trains carried passengers, freight, mail, and express in the vast area between the Great Lakes and the Pacific Ocean. At the time of the merger, the Great Northern possessed a fleet of 609 locomotives, 415 passenger cars, and 36,300 freight cars. Its principal mainlines extended from the Twin Ports of Duluth, Minnesota, and Superior, Wisconsin, and the Twin Cities of St. Paul and Minneapolis, Minnesota, to the Puget Sound on the Pacific Coast. It had more than 15,000 employees who earned over $130 million annually, and 42,000 stockholders who owned over six million individual shares.

Built in April 1945 and delivered as No. 500B, this Electro-Motive Division E7A (E-7) unit was the second dedicated passenger diesel locomotive built for the Great Northern. Used to pull the New *Empire Builder*, it was renumbered as 500C and then 502 in the early 1950s. When the Great Northern was absorbed into the Burlington Northern in 1970, it was renumbered as 9903 and repainted in Cascade Green. It's seen here in Aurora, Illinois, in 1984. *Dan Golde*

The former Great Northern, later Burlington Northern, tracks lead through Belton, Montana, and the venerable Belton Chalets are on the right. Built in 1910, the Belton Chalets were not a commercial success after additional hotels opened within the park. The Great Northern closed all of its Glacier National Park facilities during World War II, and Belton was sold in 1946 instead of being reopened. The chalets thereafter went through a variety of owners. The place operated as Peter Pence's Pizza Parlor during the 1960s, and I spent many a night hanging out there. In the 1970s and 1980s, they were owned by the Luding family who operated the former Great Northern chalets at Sperry and Granite Park. In 1997, the Belton Chalets were acquired by Andy Baxter and Cas Still, who undertook a massive remodeling effort to restore them to their original glory. *Bill Yenne*

The Burlington Northern Railroad had 24,400 miles of mainline and 1,990 locomotives destined for the new Cascade Green paint. Of these, 33 percent came from the Chicago, Burlington & Quincy, and 31 percent came from each of the two Northerns. There were 110,741 freight cars, with 66 percent equally divided between the Great Northern and the Chicago, Burlington & Quincy, and 32 percent came from the Northern Pacific. About half of the 1,284 Burlington Northern passenger cars came from the urban commuter operations of the Chicago, Burlington & Quincy, as the other roads had retired most of their passenger cars during the 1960s.

In its first decade of service, Burlington Northern's revenues rose steadily from $1.2 billion to $5 billion, with operating income increasing from $96 million

to $.5 billion. Of this, 83 percent of the revenue and 75 percent of the income was derived from the Burlington Northern Railroad. Air freight operations accounted for 11.5 percent of revenue and 7 percent of income, while petroleum and minerals accounted for 5 percent of the revenue and 15 percent of the income. By the end of its first decade, Burlington Northern operated 3,200 locomotives and 109,000 freight cars—many of them acquired after 1970—on 27,000 miles of track.

On September 22, 1995, Burlington Northern merged with the Santa Fe Pacific Corporation, the parent company of the Atchison, Topeka & Santa Fe Railway to form the Burlington Northern Santa Fe Corporation. The operational subsidiary of this new entity, the Burlington Northern & Santa Fe Railway Company, employed about 38,000 people and operated 33,000 route miles across 28 states in the western two-thirds of the United States, stretching from major Pacific Northwest and Southern California ports to the Midwest, Southeast, and Southwest, and from the Gulf of Mexico to Canada, and in two Canadian provinces. As with the Burlington Northern Railroad, the operations of Burlington Northern & Santa Fe Railway were freight operations.

As a tribute to its venerable predecessor, the new company readopted the old Great Northern *Empire Builder* color scheme for part of its motive power fleet. At the turn of the century, the old livery was back on the highline. For the first time in a generation, it was possible to stand in Marias Pass and watch locomotives chug past in the brilliant Omaha Orange, trimmed in Pullman Green, and separated by a narrow stripe of metallic gold paint. The color scheme that had made the *Empire Builder* one of the most distinctive streamliners in North America had returned to one of the most distinctive rail lines on the continent.

Omaha Orange is back! After the Burlington Northern merged with the Santa Fe Pacific Corporation in 1995 to form the Burlington Northern Santa Fe Corporation, the old *Empire Builder* paint scheme returned to the rails of the Northwest for the first time in three decades. This General Electric Dash 9 (C449) locomotive was photographed in Whitefish, Montana, shortly after the merger. A former Burlington Northern unit, this six-axle C-C locomotive is powered by a 4,500 horsepower GE 7FDL 16-cylinder turbocharged engine. *Bill Yenne*

Seven

Amtrak and Beyond

By 1970, the year that the Great Northern disappeared into the Burlington Northern merger, the era of passenger travel by privately owned railroads in the United States was essentially over. Although limited service was still available on a few of the Class I roads through the coming decades, more than a century of competing rail passenger service across the nation was over. In the face of overwhelming competition from automobiles and airlines, rail passenger service was a losing proposition, and the losses were mounting. The railroads were bailing out, and the federal government stepped in to preserve rail transportation.

In 1970, Congress passed the Rail Passenger Service Act to "relieve the railroad industry from the burden of providing ongoing passenger service and to ensure that intercity passenger rail service would continue to be a part of the national transportation system." The act created a new American railroad company that was known officially as the National Railroad Passenger Corporation, but it operated under the name Amtrak, an amalgam of the words "American" and "Track." The new railroad officially began service on May 1, 1971, when train No. 235 departed New York's Penn Station at 12:05 a.m., bound for Philadelphia. By the end of the day, Amtrak operated formerly private passenger trains across the nation. By the end of the year, the National Rail Passenger Corporation operated 184 trains to 314 end destinations.

Amtrak took over many of the great names in American rail passenger and rolling stock services, and continued to operate them under their original names. One such service was the *Empire Builder*. The Burlington Northern operated the *Empire Builder* briefly, but it gladly turned the venerable service over to Amtrak on May 1, 1971.

The Amtrak *Empire Builder* is westbound through the steep canyon of the Middle Fork of the Flathead River adjacent to Glacier National Park. *Amtrak*

Initially, Amtrak motive power was provided by the wide range of passenger equipment that it leased or purchased from the railroads whose passenger services it took over. None of these came from among the Great Northern's recent acquisitions. The SDP40s built in 1966 and the SDP45s built in 1967 all went to the Burlington Northern to be repainted from Big Sky Blue to Cascade Green. Amtrak inherited mainly older Electro-Motive Division F7 and E8 units in the 1970s because the railroads kept their newest locomotives for freight business. However, as the new public railroad gathered steam, it began to purchase new factory-fresh equip-ment, such as the General Electric Class E60 electric locomotives, mainly for use on the electrified lines on the former Pennsylvania Railroad in the Northeast Corridor.

Passenger conversions of 3,000-horsepower Electro-Motive Division SDP40 freight locomotives were among the first diesels ordered in quantity by the National Rail Passenger Corporation for use on the *Empire Builder* and other high-profile routes. Delivered through 1974, they were numbered in the 500 to 649 series. Next came the 3,000-horsepower Electro-Motive Division F40 units, which were cowled variations on the GP40 class of freight locomotive equipped with Head End Power generators. These were built between 1976 and 1981, and numbered in the series between 200 and 400. The Electro-Motive Division also sold these locomotives to a number of transit companies in the United States and Canada. The F40 marked a comprehensive effort by the National Rail Passenger Corporation to standardize their motive power during

the 1980s. The livery used by Amtrak was predominantly silver or natural metal trimmed in red, white, and blue. In the early days, the colors covered more of the surface and resulted in bright red front ends. Eventually Amtrak reduced the colors to more tastefully rendered stripes. The F40 units had a long and useful career, but most of them were withdrawn from Amtrak service by the turn of the century.

Along with motive power, the National Rail Passenger Corporation sought to acquire a standardized fleet of rolling stock. This included new stainless steel passenger cars from Budd Manufacturing and Pullman Standard, including the new double-decked Superliner cars. In 1979, the Amtrak *Empire Builder* became the

Amtrak's *Empire Builder* pulls out of Glacier Park Station on a warm summer evening in July 1995, headed by an Electro-Motive Division F40PHR. This particular locomotive was built in August 1985. *Bill Yenne*

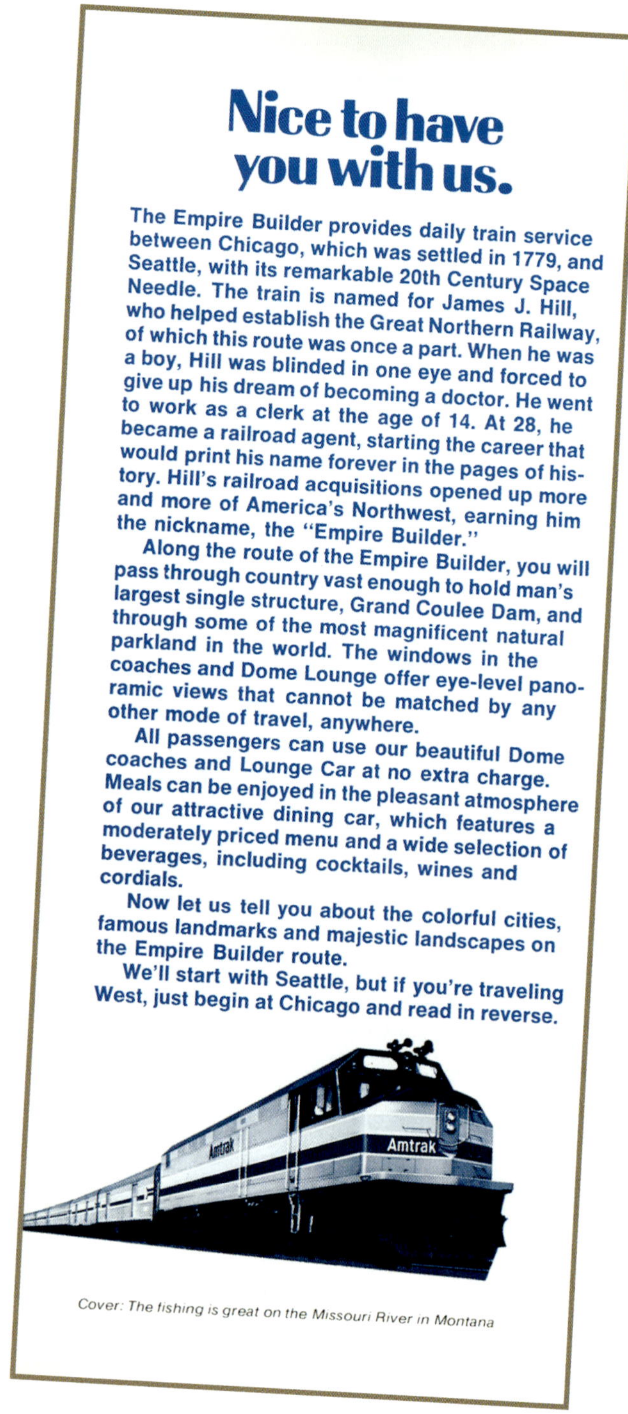

Amtrak's 1976 *Empire Builder* brochure provided passengers with the same body of information that the Great Northern did in its brochures. *Author collection*

first long-distance train in the Amtrak fleet to receive the Superliners, which had an upper-level observation deck similar to the old Budd Great Dome cars that began service with the *Empire Builder* a quarter-century before.

As for the six classic Great Dome lounge cars with the ultimate full length domes that had been part of the Mid-Century *Empire Builder*, five survived into the twenty-first century. At the turn of the century, *Glacier View* (No. 1390), which

had been retained by Burlington Northern, was still owned by the Burlington Northern Santa Fe, where it was used as a company inspection car. Of the dome cars that Amtrak took over from various roads, the venerable Great Northern *Ocean View* (No. 1391) was the last still in operation with the federal railroad. *Prairie View* (No. 1394) was in service with Holland America Westours in Alaska, and both *Mountain View* (No. 1392) and *River View* (No. 1395) were being used by the American Orient Express for its luxury rail tours of the United States.

The Amtrak *Empire Builder* heads through the Columbia River Gorge, pulled by a 1976-vintage Electro-Motive Division F40PH. During the Great Northern days, *Empire Builder* cars made this run under motive power supplied by the Spokane, Portland & Seattle Railway. *Amtrak*

Initially, the Amtrak *Empire Builder* was the only regularly scheduled passenger service between Chicago and the Pacific Northwest to survive the collapse of private sector passenger service and the takeover by the National Rail Passenger Corporation. Amtrak took the *Empire Builder* off the old Chicago, Burlington & Quincy (now Burlington Northern) line between Chicago and St. Paul, and rerouted it on the tracks of the Chicago, Milwaukee, St. Paul & Pacific (the Milwaukee Road). West of St. Paul, most of the route was on former Great Northern track as far as Sandpoint in the Idaho panhandle. From there, it rode former Northern Pacific rails to Seattle by way of Pasco and Yakima until 1981.

This is a detail of the family bedroom aboard the Superliner cars used on Amtrak's *Empire Builder*. *Amtrak*

Configured for day use, this is the economy bedroom on the original Amtrak Superliner car as used on the *Empire Builder* after 1979. *Amtrak*

Essentially all of the trackage available to Amtrak in the Pacific Northwest was now owned by the Burlington Northern.

During the 1970s, the *Empire Builder* had no service to Portland. Passengers had to travel to Seattle and change to the southbound *Coast Starlight*, a train based on former Southern Pacific service. In 1981, Amtrak undertook a major realignment precipitated by Burlington Northern's decision to downgrade the old

A compartment as seen from the hallway of an Amtrak Superliner typical of those used on the *Empire Builder* in the 1980s. *Amtrak*

Northern Pacific mainline west of Pasco. With this in mind, the National Rail Passenger Corporation decided to reroute its *Empire Builder* back to the old Great Northern mainline, now Burlington Northern–owned, from Spokane to Seattle by way of Wenatchee. Amtrak then added *Empire Builder* service into Portland by way of a run from Spokane to Pasco and through the Columbia River Gorge by way of Wishram, Washington.

For several years, the National Rail Passenger Corporation continued the *Empire Builder's* daily service, but a dearth of serviceable equipment forced the new company to reduce the schedule to four times a week in 1977. The passenger equipment that Amtrak inherited from various railroads in 1970 was already old by

The handicapped bathroom was an important feature on the Superliner cars that were introduced on Amtrak's *Empire Builder* after 1979. *Amtrak*

that time, and it was very long in the tooth by 1977. In order to allow the National Rail Passenger Corporation to continue to provide daily service between Chicago and Seattle, the *Empire Builder* was complemented by Amtrak's thrice-weekly *North Coast Hiawatha*, which operated mainly on Burlington Northern track formerly owned by the Northern Pacific, as well as on former Great Northern trackage between Spokane and Seattle. This idea of daily departures between Chicago and Seattle was short-lived as the Carter administration insisted on reducing Amtrak's long distance trains in the West. In the autumn of 1979, the government bean-counters terminated a number of such trains, including the *North Coast Hiawatha*. The *Empire Builder* was saved, but its schedule was slashed to just three days a week.

Ready to receive passengers—the coach section of an Amtrak Superliner in the 1980s. *Amtrak*

Meanwhile in 1978, the National Rail Passenger Corporation had terminated passenger service at the former Great Northern Station in Minneapolis, which had opened in 1914 and had been used by the *Empire Builder* for the entirety of its four decades as the signature train of the Great Northern. As of March 1, *Empire Builder* passengers travelling from the Twin Cities would catch their train at Amtrak's new Midway Station in St. Paul.

The abbreviated schedule was extremely unpopular, especially in the lightly populated northern tier of the Great Plains. Airline deregulation, a favorite project for Jimmy Carter when he was in the White House in the late 1970s, had adversely affected air transportation service to the more remote parts of the United States. With airlines pulling out of places such as the Dakotas for economic reasons, people depended on Amtrak more than ever, even as Carter was cutting it. North Dakota Senator Mark Andrews was instrumental in fighting for Amtrak passengers in the wide open spaces. Late in 1981, the National Rail Passenger Corporation began rebuilding the *Empire Builder* schedule back from more than two years at its all-time low of three departures weekly. For the Christmas holiday season, the *Empire Builder* ran on a daily basis with the understanding that it would revert back to the pre-season schedule after the first of the year. However, Amtrak announced in January 1982 that it would retain the daily schedule. Senator Andrews, who was chairman of the U.S. Senate Appropriations Committee, made sure the National Rail Passenger Corporation received the necessary funding. It also didn't hurt that Amtrak could demonstrate that ridership on the *Empire Builder* was up, and that the recently reinstated service to Portland added to the train's popularity and utility.

By the end of the 1980s, the F40 fleet was an average age of about a dozen years, and Amtrak wanted to bring a new-generation locomotive into the motive power fleet as a supplement and eventual replacement. Turning to General Electric Transportation Systems, Amtrak purchased a small number of P32 converted freight locomotives for delivery in 1991. Numbered in the 500 series, these were operated in the usual silver livery with red-and-blue striping. Because of the

The Amtrak *Empire Builder* passes the signals at Red Eagle, Montana, with motive power supplied by a 1981-vintage Electro-Motive Division F40PHR. *Amtrak*

undistinguished contours of the P32, the overall look of the locomotive in this color scheme reminded people of contemporary Pepsi-Cola packaging. For this reason, the Amtrak P32s were nicknamed Pepsi cans.

Amtrak's first all-new passenger motive power since the Electro-Motive Division F40 were acquired from General Electric. These were Model AMD103 Units, better known as the Genesis series. Designated by Amtrak as the Type P40, the first Genesis locomotives were delivered in 1993. The four axle B-B P40 diesels delivered 4,000 horsepower and had a design speed of 103 miles per hour. Their General Electric model number stood for "Amtrak Diesel, 103 mph."

In 1996, General Electric began delivering an improved version of the Genesis. Designated as Type P42, these diesels were generally similar to the P40 in appearance, but had a power rating of 4,200 horsepower. The P40 Genesis units were numbered in the 800 to 843 series, while the P42 Genesis units were numbered in two blocks. Numbers 1 through 120 were delivered through 1998, while numbers 121 through 207 joined the fleet through 2001. A variety of color schemes have

The Amtrak *Empire Builder* crosses the Two Medicine Bridge with the majestic mountains of Glacier National Park in the background. Built by the Great Northern at the turn of the twentieth century, the bridge is taller than a 20-story building. *Amtrak*

appeared on the Genesis locomotives, and those in the Northeast Corridor were the first to be painted with dark-blue fronts that later became standard.

Through the 1980s and into the 1990s, the National Rail Passenger Corporation operated the *Empire Builder* on a daily schedule. However, Amtrak depended upon an ongoing subsidy from the federal government. As such, it was continuously in the crosshairs of Congressional budget-cutters who complained

The Great Northern *Empire Builder* stopped at Belton, Montana, on its first run in 1929, and it is still a key Amtrak *Empire Builder* stop today. In deference to Midvale being renamed "East Glacier" with the arrival of the railroad, Belton was renamed "West Glacier" in 1949. Neverthe-less, the Great Northern, the Burlington Northern, and Amtrak continued to refer to the depot here as "Belton." Although the rest of the town has been known as "West Glacier" for over 50 years, the *Empire Builder* still stops in Belton. *Bill Yenne*

The January 1984 edition of the Amtrak *Empire Builder* onboard route guide featured a specially designed logo. Eventually, Amtrak adopted a more far-reaching branding concept for the *Empire Builder*. *Author collection*

that it should be run as a business and at a profit. Amtrak was characterized it as a boondoggle unworthy of subsidy. For this reason, Amtrak was compelled once again to reduce the *Empire Builder* schedule, down from seven to four times weekly in 1995.

The 1995 schedule was complemented by the *Pioneer*, a train that the National Rail Passenger Corporation had created in 1977 to connect Chicago

The Many Glacier Hotel, the crown jewel of the former Great Northern Glacier National Park hotel system, as it appears today. In the background are Swiftcurrent Lake and (left to right) Grinnell Point, Swiftcurrent Mountain, and Mount Wilbur. *Bill Yenne*

to the Pacific Northwest by the former Union Pacific Railroad route running through Omaha, Nebraska; Denver, Colorado; Laramie, Wyoming; and Boise, Idaho. Amtrak's idea was to provide daily service from Chicago to the Northwest by running the *Pioneer* three days a week, and the *Empire Builder* the other four. This plan remained in place for two years, but in 1997 Amtrak terminated the *Pioneer* and restored the daily schedule of the *Empire Builder* using locomotives, cars, and other equipment consolidated from the two routes.

With the *Empire Builder* finally established as Amtrak's only service between Chicago, Seattle, and Portland, the National Rail Passenger Corporation turned to marketing the train. In the 1990s, the Amtrak *Empire Builder Magazine*, an onboard magazine patterned after airline in-flight magazines, appeared on the train. It was created by OnBoard Publications of Vancouver, British Columbia, under the direction of Amtrak's Gary Erford, who was the product line director for the *Empire Builder*. To support the concept of the *Empire Builder* as a product line, a new *Empire Builder* logo was created for the National Rail Passenger Corporation by J. Craig Thorpe of Bellevue, Washington. It featured a General Electric Genesis locomotive set amid iconography reminiscent of the old Great Northern. This included a ring of Omaha Orange, trimmed in gold with Pullman Green lettering, and with Rocky the mountain goat set to one side.

Almost as soon as its hotels opened in Glacier National Park, the Great Northern Railway contracted the White Motor Company for several series of bright red buses to carry patrons from the rail stations. The Great Northern is gone now, but the 17-passenger Jammers delivered by White in 1936 and 1937 are still going strong. In 2001, the Ford Motor Company rehabilitated 32 of the 33 buses with new chassis, wiring, and a dual propane/gasoline fuel system. One will be kept as close as possible to original condition for historical purposes. Many Glacier Hotel and Allen Mountain are in the background. *Bill Yenne*

In 1996, Amtrak extended its Interpretive Guides Program to the *Empire Builder*. Having existed previously on such Amtrak trains as the *Southwest Chief*, the program was created to familiarize passengers with local history and natural history by putting local guides aboard the trains to point out features in the country the train passed through. The *Empire Builder* Interpretive Guides rode the train from Edmonds, Washington, just north of Seattle across the continent, past Glacier National Park to Shelby, Montana. They were sponsored by the Great Northern Railway Historical Society from 1996 through 2000, and then the service became a joint activity of the National Rail Passenger Corporation and the National Park Service. The guides were volunteers from the Klondike Gold Rush

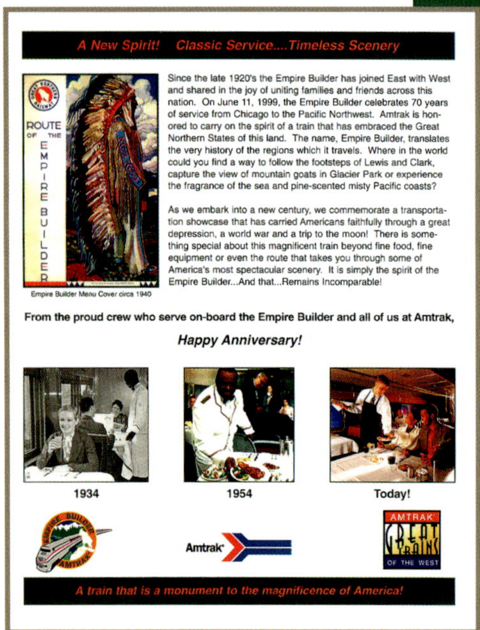

A New Spirit! Classic Service....Timeless Scenery

Since the late 1920's the Empire Builder has joined East with West and shared in the joy of uniting families and friends across this nation. On June 11, 1999, the Empire Builder celebrates 70 years of service from Chicago to the Pacific Northwest. Amtrak is honored to carry on the spirit of a train that has embraced the Great Northern States of this land. The name, Empire Builder, translates the very history of the regions which it travels. Where in the world could you find a way to follow the footsteps of Lewis and Clark, capture the view of mountain goats in Glacier Park or experience the fragrance of the sea and pine-scented misty Pacific coasts?

As we embark into a new century, we commemorate a transportation showcase that has carried Americans faithfully through a great depression, a world war and a trip to the moon! There is something special about this magnificent train beyond fine food, fine equipment or even the route that takes you through some of America's most spectacular scenery. It is simply the spirit of the Empire Builder...And that...Remains Incomparable!

Empire Builder Menu Cover circa 1940

From the proud crew who serve on-board the Empire Builder and all of us at Amtrak,

Happy Anniversary!

1934 1954 Today!

A train that is a monument to the magnificence of America!

In 1999, Amtrak paid tribute to the history of the *Empire Builder* with this special dining car menu. Commissioned by Charles Mott of the Washington Association of Rail Passengers, the cover painting by J. Craig Thorpe depicts important moments in *Empire Builder* history. Clockwise from the top, we see an Amtrak P42 locomotive pulling the train over Marias Pass with Little Dog and Summit Mountain in the background; Amtrak Superliners meeting a red bus at Glacier Park Station; a Great Northern *Empire Builder* passing the Isaac Walton Inn at Essex, Montana; a pair of Rocky Mountain goats, the *Empire Builder's* totem animal; and a steam era *Empire Builder* pulling into the Belton Depot. Note the Winold Reiss painting on the back cover (inset). *J. Craig Thorpe*

National Historical Park, which was based in Seattle. As described by the Park Service, these volunteer Interpretive Guides provided narration as the *Empire Builder* "meanders through fabulous vistas of the Cascade Mountains, the arid, fruit-bearing desert region of eastern Washington, the southern border of breathtaking Glacier National Park, and the expansive prairie country of western and central Montana."

Glacier National Park continued to be the key vacation destination on the *Empire Builder*. Amtrak found itself selling the park just as the Great Northern had. As it was the case a half-century before, Glacier National Park is still featured more prominently than any other location in the marketing of the *Empire Builder*.

This is the Summer 1998 issue of *Empire Builder Magazine*. As the streamliner approached its seventh decade of service, Amtrak undertook a major marketing effort, including creating a logo and this onboard magazine for passengers. The logo was designed by J. Craig Thorpe. *Courtesy of Dan Engstrom, Amtrak*

Railfans certainly chuckled at the sight of the tag line of the Winter 1998–1999 issue of *Empire Builder Magazine*. "America's Great Northern Adventure" paid tribute to the railway that created the *Empire Builder*. *Courtesy of Dan Engstrom, Amtrak*

Although they presented an ongoing maintenance challenge, the four grand hotels of Glacier and Waterton continued to be just as popular in the twenty-first century as they had been when Louis Warren Hill created them in the early twentieth century. When Louis had passed away in 1948, the Great Northern started to explore divesting itself of its Glacier Park Company and the management responsibility of these properties. The Great Northern had continued in the role until the 1957 season when the management contract went to Minneapolis construction company executive Donald Knutson. The railroad sweetened the deal by underwriting the cost of a massive remodelling project. Losses suffered by Knutson's management organization led to the contract not being renewed. The hotels were sold to the National Park Service and the management was taken over in 1960 by

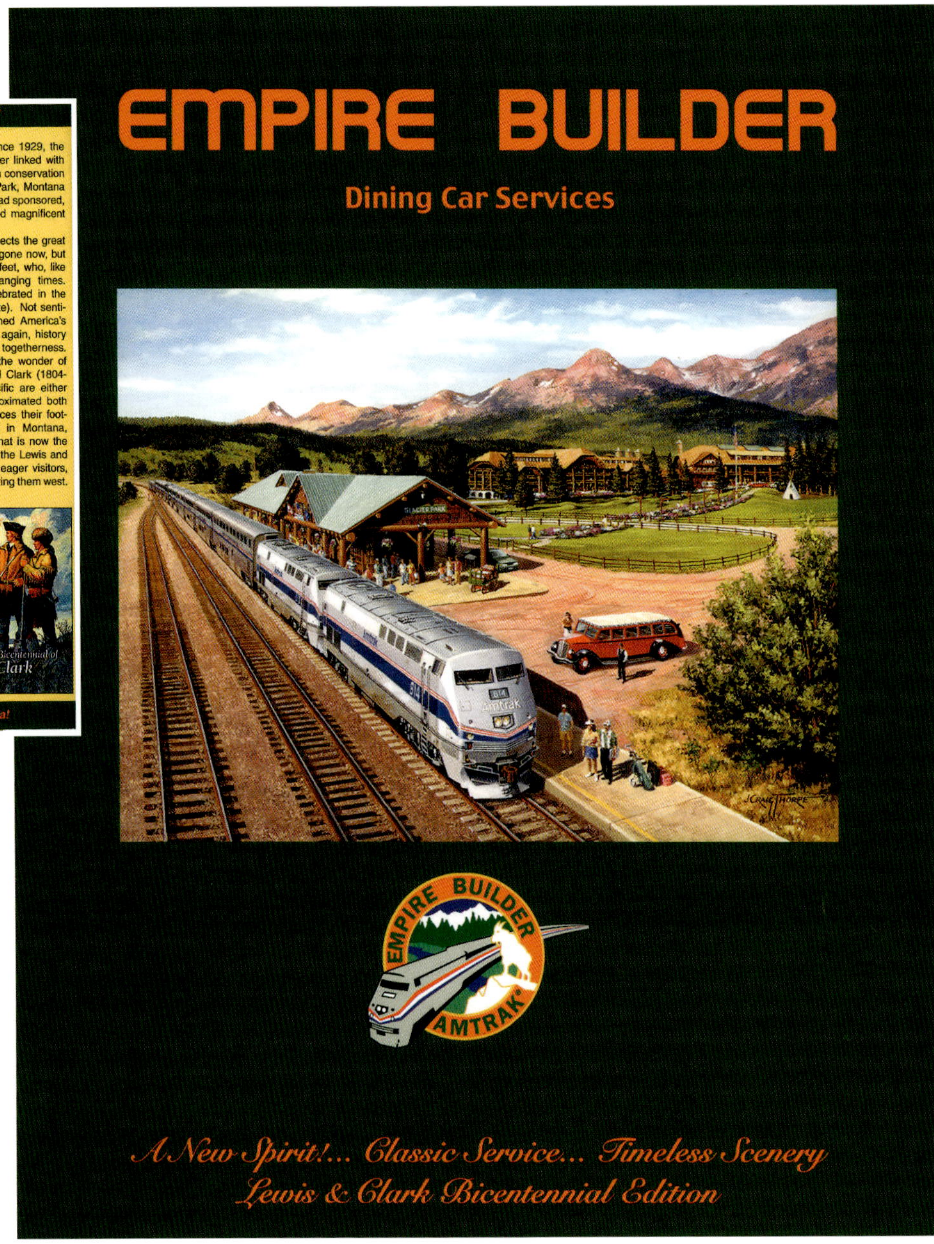

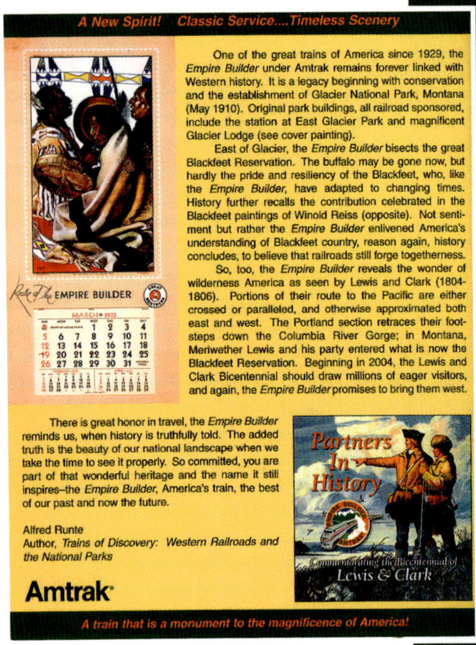
A New Spirit! Classic Service....Timeless Scenery

One of the great trains of America since 1929, the *Empire Builder* under Amtrak remains forever linked with Western history. It is a legacy beginning with conservation and the establishment of Glacier National Park, Montana (May 1910). Original park buildings, all railroad sponsored, include the station at East Glacier Park and magnificent Glacier Lodge (see cover painting).

East of Glacier, the *Empire Builder* bisects the great Blackfeet Reservation. The buffalo may be gone now, but hardly the pride and resiliency of the Blackfeet, who, like the *Empire Builder*, have adapted to changing times. History further recalls the contribution celebrated in the Blackfeet paintings of Winold Reiss (opposite). Not sentiment but rather the *Empire Builder* enlivened America's understanding of Blackfeet country, reason again, history concludes, to believe that railroads still forge togetherness.

So, too, the *Empire Builder* reveals the wonder of wilderness America as seen by Lewis and Clark (1804-1806). Portions of their route to the Pacific are either crossed or paralleled, and otherwise approximated both east and west. The Portland section retraces their footsteps down the Columbia River Gorge; in Montana, Meriwether Lewis and his party entered what is now the Blackfeet Reservation. Beginning in 2004, the Lewis and Clark Bicentennial should draw millions of eager visitors, and again, the *Empire Builder* promises to bring them west.

There is great honor in travel, the *Empire Builder* reminds us, when history is truthfully told. The added truth is the beauty of our national landscape when we take the time to see it properly. So committed, you are part of that wonderful heritage and the name it still inspires–the *Empire Builder*, America's train, the best of our past and now the future.

Alfred Runte
Author, *Trains of Discovery: Western Railroads and the National Parks*

Amtrak

A train that is a monument to the magnificence of America!

For the front cover of this commemorative-edition *Empire Builder* dining car menu, Amtrak commissioned J. Craig Thorpe to paint the *Empire Builder* at Glacier Park Station. In his painting titled *Wilderness Threshold*, Thorpe depicted an 11-car *Empire Builder* pulled by a pair of General Electric P40 Genesis locomotives, meeting a former Great Northern Jammer bus. The artist and his wife are on the platform at the far right. Note the Winold Reiss painting on the back cover (inset). *J. Craig Thorpe*

the Arizona-based Glacier Park, Incorporated, founded by entrepreneur Don Hummel. After two decades under Hummel's leadership, Glacier Park, Incorporated, was sold to Greyhound Food Management in 1981, which in turn became a division of the Viad Corporation.

In June 2004, Amtrak pulled out the stops to celebrate the 75th Anniversary of the *Empire Builder*. The festivities began on June 11 with events held at the King Street Station in Seattle and at Portland Union Station. Montana's Governor Judy Martz, boarded the westbound *Empire Builder* at Havre, Montana, on June 12 to ride the train into Seattle to join in the ongoing celebration.

By the middle of the twentieth century, the *Empire Builder* had become a cultural icon and is a part of the history of its corner of the continent where it had

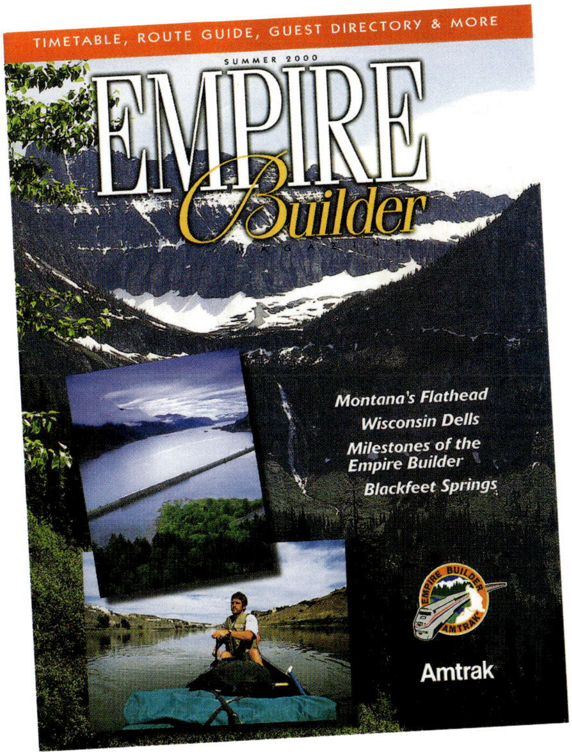

The Summer 2000 edition of Amtrak's onboard *Empire Builder Magazine* pays tribute to the many sights enjoyed by passengers, including the Montana Rockies. *Courtesy of Dan Engstrom, Amtrak*

In the winter, the *Empire Builder* becomes a ski train. With Montana's airports subject to delays and cancellations during the snowy winter months, taking the *Empire Builder* is often the best way to get to the slopes. *Courtesy of Dan Engstrom, Amtrak*

The *Empire Builder* was featured on the cover of Amtrak's 2003–2004 system-wide travel guide. The motive power pictured here includes a General Electric P40 Genesis in the lead and a newer P42 Genesis behind. The P40s were in the 800-series, while the P42 nomenclature started at Number 1. *Courtesy of Dan Engstrom, Amtrak*

achieved immortality. As we said in the introduction, this book is the story of a man, his railroad, and that railroad's signature train.

Jim Hill died in 1916, but he lived on in the form of the Great Northern, a railroad that he had practically built by hand. The Great Northern itself passed away in 1970, but it lives on in the form of the *Empire Builder*, the train the railroad created in celebration of its founder.

The train has achieved immortality and has assured the immortality of the memory of the man and his railroad. This book has been the story, but only part of the story, for it continues to be written to this day.

The conductor helps a passenger alight from a Superliner. This Amtrak *Empire Builder* makes its westbound 12:26 p.m. stop in Glasgow, Montana, 1,211 route miles out of Chicago, during its 75th Anniversary in June 2004. *Bill Yenne*

Taxis line up at Seattle's King Street Station to meet Amtrak *Empire Builder* passengers. The Puget Sound Transit commuter trains, the Sounders, as well as Amtrak, make use of the venerable old monument. Remodeled in the 1940s and again for the 1962 Seattle World's Fair, the station's original ornate ceiling was covered by art deco plaster walls and ceiling tiles. Beginning in 2003, a major restoration brought back some of the lost magnificence and turned the old station into an important transit hub. *Bill Yenne*

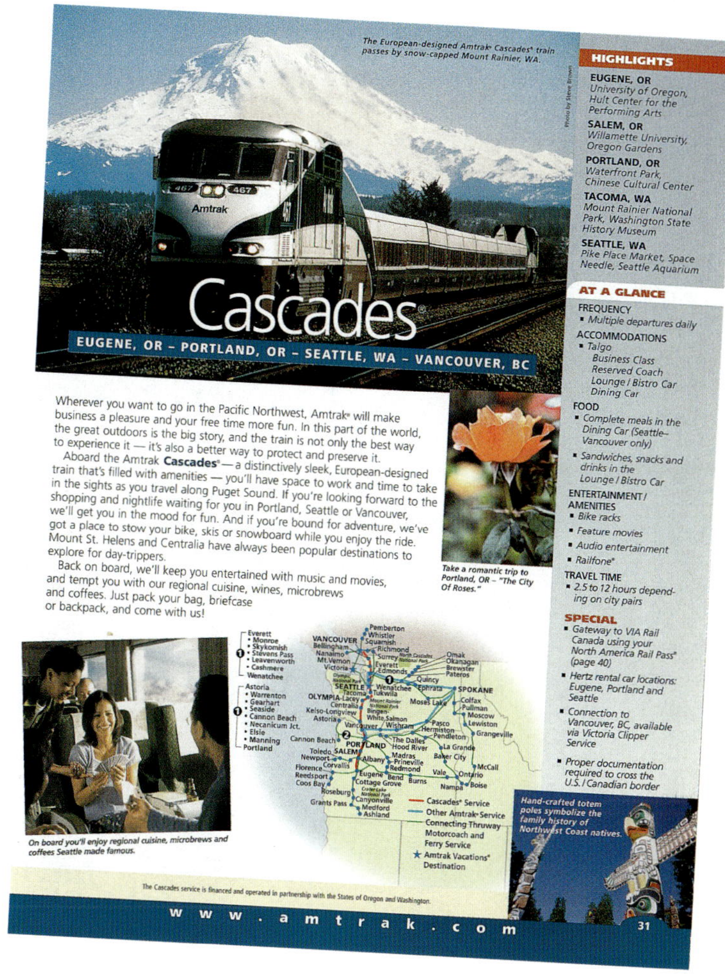

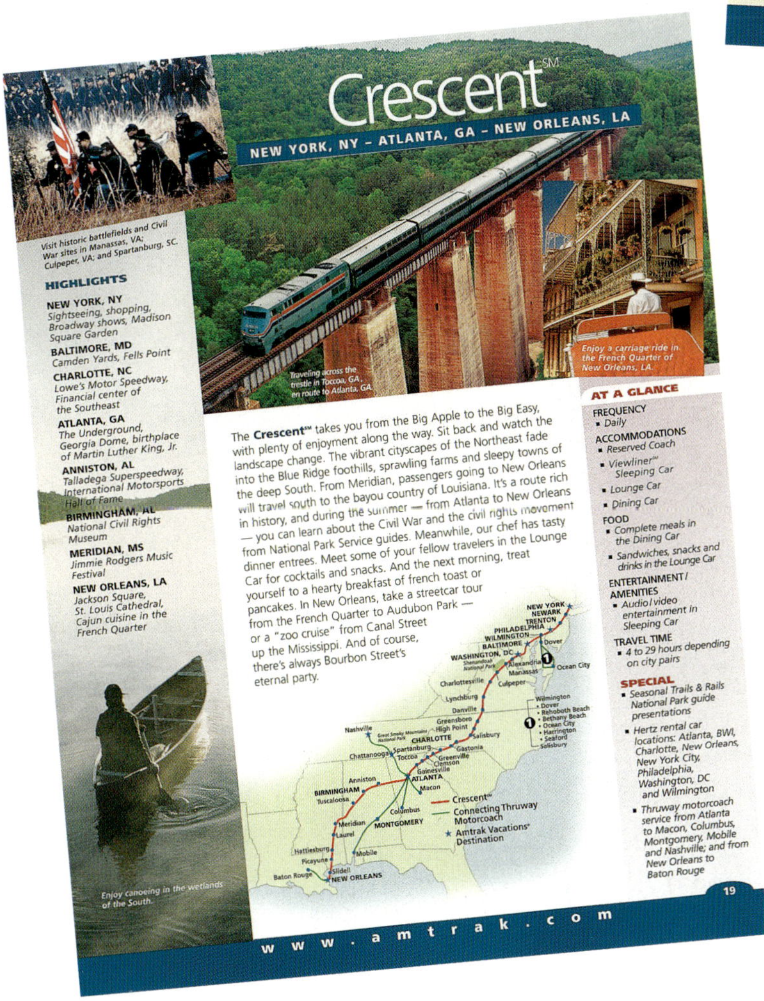

The *Empire Builder* warrants a two-page spread in the Amtrak system-wide travel guide. These pages provide a good overview of *Empire Builder* service as it existed early in the twenty-first century. *Courtesy of Dan Engstrom, Amtrak*

EMPIRE BUILDER

Chicago • St. Paul • Portland/Seattle

7	◄ Train Number ►					8
Daily	◄ Days of Operation ►					Daily
R 🛏 🍽 ☕ 🎥 🚭	◄ On Board Service ►					R 🛏 🍽 ☕ 🎥 🚭
Read Down	Mile	▼		Symbol	▲	Read Up
2 10P	0	Dp	Chicago, IL–Union Sta. (CT)	💼 ♿ ✸ ●	Ar	3 45P
R 2 34P	18		Glenview, IL (METRA/Milw. Line)	♿ ●		D 3 05P
R 3 50P	86		Milwaukee, WI	💼 ♿ ●		D 2 05P
5 00P	150		Columbus, WI (Madison)	💼 ♿ ●		12 35P
5 29P	178		Portage, WI	♿		12 05P
5 47P	195		Wisconsin Dells, WI	♿		11 47A
6 25P	240		Tomah, WI	♿		11 06A
7 11P	281		La Crosse, WI	♿ ●		10 25A
7 44P	308		Winona, MN	♿ ●		9 49A
8 46P	371		Red Wing, MN	♿		8 44A
10 25P 11 15P	417	Ar Dp	St. Paul-Minneapolis, MN 🚌 Duluth—see at right	💼 ♿ ✸ ●	Dp Ar	7 40A 7 05A
12 40A	482		St. Cloud, MN	♿		5 11A
1 42A	548		Staples, MN			4 06A
2 38A	610		Detroit Lakes, MN			3 07A
3 49A	658		Fargo, ND (Moorhead)	💼 ♿ ●		2 10A
5 04A	732		Grand Forks, ND	💼 ♿ ●		12 54A
6 25A	817		Devils Lake, ND	♿		11 32P
7 19A	874		Rugby, ND	⊘ ♿		10 38P
8 46A 9 06A	935	Ar Dp	Minot, ND	💼 ♿ ●	Dp Ar	9 42P 9 22P
9 57A	989		Stanley, ND	♿		8 11P
11 07A	1055		Williston, ND (CT)	⊘ ♿		7 09P
11 41A	1162		Wolf Point, MT (MT)	⊘ ♿		4 33P
12 26P	1211		Glasgow, MT	♿		3 47P
1 25P	1277		Malta, MT	♿		2 52P
2 39P 3 04P	1366	Ar Dp	Havre, MT	💼 ♿ ●	Dp Ar	1 32P 1 12P
5 22P	1471		Shelby, MT (Great Falls, Butte 🚌)	💼 ♿ ●		11 43A
5 51P	1495		Cut Bank, MT	♿		10 45A
41	1528		Browning, MT			41
40 6 45P	1542		East Glacier Park, MT	♿ ✸ ●		40 9 54A
⚒ 7 41P	1573		Essex, MT–Izaak Walton Inn	✸		⚒ 8 55A
8 23P	1599		West Glacier, MT (Apgar)	✸		8 16A
8 56P 9 16P	1620	Ar Dp	Whitefish, MT (Kalispell)	💼 ♿ ✸ ●		7 46A 7 26A
10 59P	1723	Dp	Libby, MT (MT)	♿		5 41A
11 49P	1807		Sandpoint, ID (PT)	♿		2 47A
1 40A	1877	Ar	Spokane, WA (Coeur d'Alene, ID)	💼 ♿ ●	Dp	1 15A
27			Thru Cars Chicago–Portland			28
2 45A	1877	Dp	Spokane, WA	💼 ♿ ●	Ar	12 13A
5 35A	2025		Pasco, WA (Kennewick, Richland)	💼 ♿ ●		8 57P
7 30A	2151		Wishram, WA (The Dalles)	♿		6 55P
8 04A	2182		Bingen-White Salmon, WA	♿		6 21P
9 20A	2247		Vancouver, WA	💼 ♿ ●		5 07P
39 10 10A	2257	Ar	Portland, OR (PT)	💼 ♿ ✸ ●	Dp	39 4 45P
2 15A	1877	Dp	Spokane, WA	💼 ♿ ●	Ar	12 32A
4 38A	1996		Ephrata, WA	♿		9 42P
5 43A	2048		Wenatchee, WA	♿		8 42P
8 41A	2173		Everett, WA	💼 ♿ ●		5 44P
9 08A	2188		Edmonds, WA	💼 ♿ ●		5 17P
10 20A	2206	Ar	Seattle, WA (Victoria, BC ⛴) (PT) 🚌 Vancouver, BC—see at right	💼 ♿ ✸ ●	Dp	4 45P

West

Symbols and Reference Marks

- **D** Stops only to discharge passengers.
- **R** Stops only to receive passengers.
- ⚒ Stops only on signal, or advance notice to conductor.
- 19 Passengers not carried locally between this station and Chicago except when connecting at Chicago to/from other Amtrak® trains.
- 36 Direct transfer between train and motorcoach at Amtrak® station for connecting passengers only.
- 39 Connections available to/from Salem, Albany and Eugene-Springfield. See page 101 for schedule.
- 40 East Glacier Park Station will be open May 1 through October 5, 2004.
- 41 Browning Station will re-open October 6, 2004.

Services on the Empire Builder

- R **Coaches: Reservations required**
- 🛏 **Sleeping Cars:** First Class Superliner® Service
  - Amtrak®'s Metropolitan Lounge® available in Chicago and Portland for First Class Service passengers
- 🍽 **Dining Car:** Complete meals
  - Not available between Spokane and Portland; First Class passengers will receive complimentary cold meal service
- ☕ **Sightseer Lounge:** Sandwiches, snacks and beverages (**Note**—Combined Diner/Lounge provides food and beverage service between Spokane and Seattle)
- 🎥 **Entertainment:** Feature movies offered between Chicago and Portland.
  Trails and Rails Program: In a cooperative effort with the National Park Service, volunteer rangers provide narrative along the route (Spring/Summer).
- 🚭 **Smoking:** Smoking is prohibited entirely on this train. Passengers may smoke on station platforms as announced by train crews, and must remain next to the train, ready to board immediately upon hearing the locomotive horn and verbal "All Aboard" calls.

Scenic Highlights

- Wisconsin Dells
- Mississippi River
- Rocky Mountains
- Glacier National Park, Montana
- Gateway to Mount Rainier, Washington
- Columbia River Gorge

Amtrak is proud to commemorate the 75th anniversary of the Empire Builder and the 200th anniversary of the Lewis & Clark Expedition.

Empire Builder 75th anniversary posters featuring this illustration are available at www.amtrak.com/store.

Connecting Local Services

Shelby–Great Falls–Helena–Butte

Rimrock Stages operates service between Amtrak®'s Shelby Station and Great Falls, Helena and Butte, MT. Purchase ticket from Rimrock Stages. (406) 453-1541.

Thruway Motorcoach Connections

NOTE—Greyhound schedules subject to change

Duluth • St. Paul/Minneapolis *(Greyhound Lines)*

8007		▼	Thruway Number		▲	8008
5 25P	*0*	Dp	*Duluth, MN (CT)*		Ar	*11 20A*
5 45P			*Cloquet, MN*			*10 55A*
6 40P			*Sandstone, MN*			*10 00A*
8 05P	*149*	Ar	*St. Paul-Minneapolis, MN –Amtrak® Sta. (CT)*	●	Dp	*8 25A*

Seattle • Vancouver, BC *(Western Trailways)*

8948		▼	Thruway Number		▲	8909
10 45A	*0*	Dp	*Seattle, WA (PT)*	♿ ✸ ●	Ar	*4 30P*
D *1 15P*	*115*		*Surrey, BC–Pacific Inn*			R *1 30P*
D *1 45P*	*132*		*Richmond, BC–Delta Pacific Resort*			R *1 00P*
2 15P	*144*	Ar	*Vancouver, BC –Pacific Central Sta. (PT)*	♿ ✸ ●	Dp	*12 30P*

California Zephyr Track Work

To accommodate track maintenance being performed by the UP in June and July, the California Zephyr will require some detours. On certain dates, the train will operate through Wyoming, bypassing the Moffat Tunnel and Colorado River Gorge. Go to www.amtrak.com or call 1-800-USA-RAIL for schedule adjustments in June and July, 2004.

88

For Amtrak® reservations, visit www.amtrak.com or call 1-800-USA-RAIL

This *Empire Builder* timetable provides an overview of *Empire Builder* operations at the time that the great train celebrated its 75th Anniversary. *Courtesy of Dan Engstrom, Amtrak*

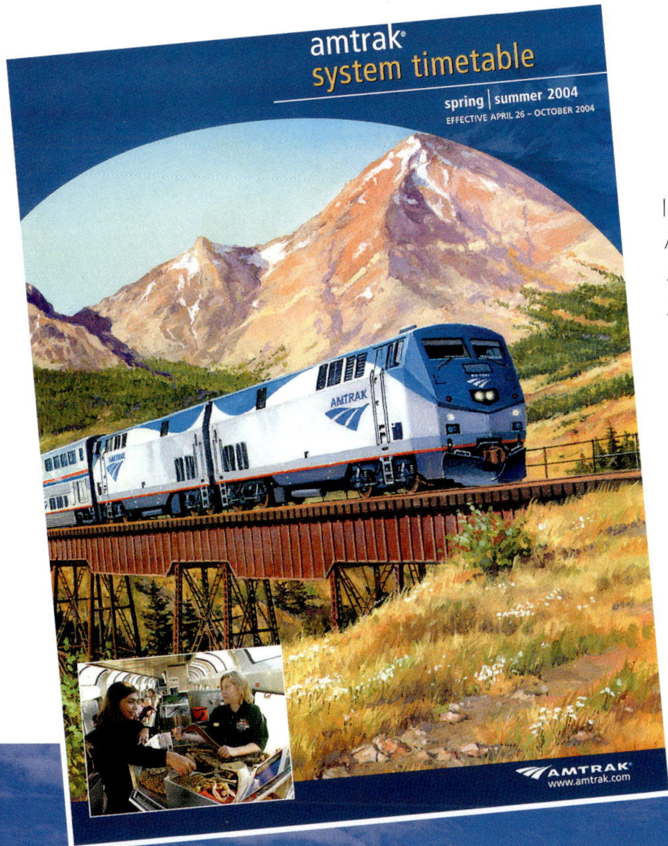

In anticipation of the *Empire Builder's* 75th Anniversary, Charles Mott of the Washington Association of Rail Passengers commissioned J. Craig Thorpe to create this painting of a pair of a Bluenose General Electric Genesis P42s pulling the train across the Two Medicine Bridge near Glacier National Park. In turn,the painting was reproduced by Amtrak on the cover of their system-wide timetable that coincided with the *Empire Builder* 75th Anniversary celebration. *J. Craig Thorpe*

The Amtrak *Empire Builder* rolls into Whitefish, Montana, pulled by a pair of General Electric Genesis P42s. The lead locomotive was delivered to the railroad in 1997 with the original red, white, and blue striping seen here, but after its 2002 overhaul it was repainted in Amtrak's twenty-first century Bluenose livery. *Bill Yenne*

Index

1800